T0129763

Jesus Christ
SPEAKS TO THE
Present Day Church

DR. JOHN THOMAS WYLIE

authorHOUSE®

AuthorHouse™
1663 Liberty Drive
Bloomington, IN 47403
www.authorhouse.com
Phone: 1 (800) 839-8640

Published by AuthorHouse 11/25/2019

ISBN: 978-1-7283-3766-1 (sc)
ISBN: 978-1-7283-3765-4 (e)

Print information available on the last page.

Scripture quotations marked KJV are from the Holy Bible, King James Version (Authorized Version). First published in 1611. Quoted from the KJV Classic Reference Bible, Copyright © 1983 by The Zondervan Corporation.

Scripture quotations marked RSV are taken from the Revised Standard Version of the Bible, copyright © 1946, 1952, 1971 by the Division of Christian Education of the National Council of the Churches of Christ in the USA. Used by permission.

American Standard Version (ASV)
Public Domain

The Holy Bible (1959) The Berkeley Version. Grand Rapids, MI.: Zondervan (Used By Permission)

This book is printed on acid-free paper.

Contents

Foreword

IN A TIME (TODAY) when men and false teachers go ahead from terrible to worse, beguiling and being betrayed (II Timothy 3:13 KJV), God's people ought to be moved to a more profound, spiritual sanctification and worship in their every day conduct (II Peter 3:11). The more evil the hour, the holier ought to be the yearnings and conduct of Christians.

Such is the call of God in these evil, terrible, and troublesome times. The letter to the seven churches of Asia Minor interpretation of new power as we tune in to the Son of Man speaking through them to the churches of our present day. The fact that what our Lord said includes about one-eighth of the Book of the Revelation serves to stress the significance God puts on these encouragements and warnings.

The application is made to the present century in which God needs progressively steadfast, faithful men and women to call the Body of Christ to repentance. Here is superb reading material for Christians and Christian laborers in circumstances and times such as these.

This investigation will help stir us to a serious acknowledgment that it is later than we might suspect. We will be moved to ask and fill in as at no other time, looking with sure desire for some souls before the great and terrible day of the Lord shall come.

Reverend Dr. John Thomas Wylie

Chapter One

Who Is This Christ?

THE PERSON WHO ADDRESS Himself to the seven churches in the Book of Revelation painstakingly examines their different records, looking at their outward activities, as well as testing to the plain heart of the intentions inciting their activities. He directions, empowers, educates, cautions, and censures wherever fundamental.

The inquiry normally emerges, Who is He? Has He the privilege to talk as He does? Has He the power to complete His promises and warnings? This isn't a light issue to consider, in light of the fact that the position and character of the person who talks in such a circumstance as this sets up the weight to be joined to his words.

In the first chapter of the Book of the Revelation John portrayed this Person as the "Son of Man." He is seen standing amidst the lampstands, knowing to the last detail what is coming to pass among the churches.

His name, the "Son of Man," is the most used by Jesus Christ amid His public ministry. The name depicts Him as the representative man and assigns Him as the last Adam in contrast to the first man, Adam (I Cor. 15:45 KJV).

He is the Eternal Son of God, Creator, and Sustainer of the universe. But, His other name, Son of Man, serves to distinguish Him as the One who gave Himself as the sacrifice to save men.

Christ is thus put forward as Judge. Be that as it may, He is the High Priestly Judge who takes disciplinary measures with His people as He affectionately looks to manage them in the ways of truth. This is as opposed to His situation as Kingly Judge in the twentieth chapter of Revelation where He controls punitive justice to the individuals who have rejected all endeavors to reconcile them to God.

As High Priestly Judge He uncovered the wrongdoings (sins) and pitiable state of His people through uncovering His very own perfection and beauty and holiness. What's more, it is additionally as High Priestly Judge that He can state, "I am he that liveth, and was dead; and, observe, I am alive for evermore" (Rev. 1:18).

As a Royal Judge in Revelation 20 He doesn't offer redemption to the individuals who show up before Him at the Great White Throne judgment. The season of probation will then have been finished.

As the High holy Judge He walks amidst the places of worship; however as the Kingly Judge He will sit on His royal throne and articulate last sentence against all who have rejected God's offer of leniency (mercy).

It is with the High Priestly Judge, at that point, that we are worried as we look to find what the Scriptures say concerning Him who addresses the congregation.

The apostle discloses to us that he turned to see the voice that spoke with him and found "amidst the seven candles one like unto the "Son of Man," dressed with an article of clothing down to the foot, and girt about the paps with a brilliant support" (Rev. 1:13). What Christ needed to state was not a matter of hearsay on His part, for He stood amidst the churches. There was nothing that escaped Him.

Righteous

We see in this depiction, as a matter of first importance, that He was completely dressed (fully clothed). He speaks of His absolute holiness. This is rather than Adam who, when he trespassed (sinned), gotten himself stripped, naked. It is additionally as opposed to the time when Christ came to die for men and was disrobed and crucified on the cross as a result of the spiritual nakedness of man.

In any case, now that is altogether changed. He is imagined here as the "Sinless One," the One who is flawless, perfect, completely heavenly, absolutely holy. There are no fig leaves here, for example, our first parents wore however apparel that reaches to His feet. He is the one preceding whom each person will one day have to stand. They will see Him as He is here, flawless, perfect and glorious in His righteousness.

Absolute Divine Authority

Furthermore, we discover Him girded with a golden girdle which is an symbol of absolute divine authority. Jesus communicated this to His disciples before His ascension when he stated, "All

power is given unto me in paradise and in earth."
Go ye consequently, and show all countries,
baptizing them in the name of the Father, and of
the Son, and of the Holy Ghost; Teaching them to
observe all things whatsoever I have commanded
you: and, lo, I am with you alway, even unto
the end of the world" (Matt. 28:18-20 KJV)."
His power is with the end goal that nobody can
effectively move it.

This is completely affirmed in Scripture where
we discover that God has raised Him from the
dead and put Him far over all realms and control
and may and territory and each name that is
named, in this age, as well as in that which is to
come. God has put everything under His feet and
has offered Him to be "Head" over all things to
the church. There is none other like Him.

In Philippians chapter two, we perused:
"Wherefore God also hath highly exalted very
him, and given him a name which is above each
name: That at the name of Jesus each knee should
bow, of things in paradise, and things in earth,
and things under the earth; And that each tongue
should confess that Jesus Christ is Lord, to the
glory of God the Father" (vv. 9-11).

So great, at that point, and supreme, absolute is His power, that none can disclaim Him. Jesus has bunches of holy angels to call upon to uphold His directions if the need ought to emerge; yet so great is His power that His own Word is adequate. This is the Son of Man who speaks to the church.

Respect

Daniel 7:9 says, "I observed till the thrones were thrown down, and the Ancient of days did sit, whose piece of clothing was white as snow, and the hair of his heard like unadulterated fleece. RSV" The Son of Man is to be regarded. The wisdom of the ages is in Him. He is the Eternal One who is all wise. He is the Eternal One who was before all things and without Whose power and presence in the universe nothing would hold together.

Paul portrays Jesus Christ in these words: "Who is the image of the imperceptible God, the firstborn of every creature: For by him were all things made, that are in paradise, and that are in earth, unmistakable and undetectable, regardless of whether they be thrones, or territories, or realms, or forces: all things were made by Him, and for Him: And he is before all things, and by Him everything comprise.

He is the head of the body, the church; who is the beginning, the firstborn from the dead; that in everything he may have the superiority" (Col. 1:15-18 KJV). It is an exceedingly genuine issue (serious matter) for any individual to daintily throw away the words of Christ to whom God has given the pre-eminent place in the universe.

All-Seeing

As John proceeds with his depiction of the Son of Man He discloses to us that "his eyes were as a flames of fire" (Rev. 1:1-14 KJV). His infiltrating look sees the plain considerations and aims of men's souls. There is nothing escaped (hid) from Him. An outline may help here, however it is nevertheless a poor representation of the astounding powers our Lord has.

The X-ray machine is generally utilized today both in industry and prescription (medicine). Where the human eye could undoubtedly be deceived with respect to valuable jewels, for example, precious stones, the X-ray isn't. To the man who realizes how to utilize it, the X-ray machine reveals whether a stone is a real jewel or an impersonation.

The eyes of the Lord see much more than any X-ray at any point made by man. "I the Lord look through the heart; I attempt the reins even to give each man as indicated by his courses and as per the product of his doings." The Lord sees the thought processes back of the considerable number of activities. In addition to the fact that He knows what is done outwardly He knows the rousing standards within. We do well to hear him who speaks to the Church.

Judge

In verse 15 of Revelation 1 we find that the feet of the Son of Man are compared as "unto fine brass, as though they burned in a furnace." Brass talks about judgment. He, who used to be made a decision for man's transgression (sin), now is uncovered as the rightful Judge (Phil. 2:5-11 ASV).

His face is depicted as the sun shining in his strength. His face mirrors the glory of God. There will be no question referred to in that day as to His personality.

Nothing can stand before the brightness of His presence: "And the devil that misled them (deceived them) was thrown into the lake of fire and brimstone, where the beast and the false prophet are, and shall be tormented day and night for ever and ever. I saw a great white throne, and him that sat on it (this is the Lord Jesus), from whose face the earth and the paradise fled away; and there was discovered no place for them."

When he came the first occasion when, He came in all meekness and lowliness. He was not perceived to be the glorious Son of God, and men crucified Him.

His face was so marred, Isaiah lets us know, that it didn't resemble the essence of a man. However, when He comes the second time, He won't have a marred face but a face of glory that will outshine the sun.

It will be a face from which the heaven and earth will flee. They won't have the capacity to stand its brightness. Neither will you nor I have the capacity to stand in His presence except if we are joined to Him now. He is One to be respected.

His Word Is Final

We are next informed that His voice resembles the sound of numerous waters. However, more than sound is incorporated here, for His voice is one of power. We gain from Genesis 1 that God spake and it was so. Everything complies with His voice. Men have and even yet, oppose Him, however that is just for a period. They may even send rockets into the sky and brag that there is no God since researchers have not possessed the capacity to discover Him with their instruments.

God will enable man to achieve the finish of his resources and will then advance in and uncover Himself. He will talk with a voice that sounds like that of numerous waters, and men will tremble before Him.

When our Lord Jesus walked this world, He went to the grave of Lazarus and called: "Lazarus, come forth." Someone has admirably said that if our Lord Jesus had not assigned who was to approach the entire burial ground would have come forth.

When He returns once more, the dead will hear His voice and trusting holy people will be raised into His presence and living holy people will be made up for lost time together with them to meet the Lord in the air.

One more day will come when whatever remains of the dead will live, the individuals who have not confided in Christ as Savior, and they will stand before His Great White Throne (Rev. 20:12 KJV). His Word is last. The law was given that each mouth may be halted. His Word we are told is perpetually settled in paradise. Paradise and earth will pass away, but His Word will never pass away.

In this association we discover that out of His mouth continues a two-edged sword. The hugeness of this is proposed in Isaiah 55:11: "So will my statement be that goeth forward out of my mouth: it will not return unto me void, but rather it will thrive in the thing whereto I sent it."

God's Word continues from Him as well as comes back to Him having achieved its purpose.

In addressing the Pharisees our Savior stated, "Ye have the word, and the words that I have spoken, they will Judge you." Words that are expressions of kindness today will be expressions of judgment at a future date.

As we have stated, His words are last. There will be no natural court to translate or confound what He says. This is the Person who speaks to the present day Church.

We discover that everything is to be put under His feet. This will be a last judgment. At the point when Joshua was in procedure of repressing Canaan, five kings who had contradicted him were brought before him, and he put his foot on their necks. This connotes his position and right of judgment over them. We read of our Lord in I Corinthians 15 that all adversaries will be put under His feet. The One who was judged for our transgressions (sin) on the cross will at that point stand forward as the rightful Judge of all the earth (Phil. 2:5-11 KJV).

He is depicted as the First and the Last. It was by His Word that everything came to have being. It is by His Word that all things will be fulfilled. Men in their absurdity and insidiousness are attempting urgently to deny that Christ is Creator, along these lines planning to get away from the last judgment He has let us know will fall upon unregenerate men.

Their insidious creative impulses, in any case, will never substitute for the certainties of God; and however men attempt energetically, they can't get away from the punishment of their sin.

Dr. John Thomas Wylie

He stands as victor over all the earth. He was dead and is alive forevermore. Not even death could hold Him. Such power does not belong to men in this world. Regardless of the amazing advances made in therapeutic science in our day, the most men can do is at times prolong life, but they can't oust death. All men die, after death is the judgment.

Having become alive once again, Christ presently holds the keys to damnation (Hades) and death. Jesus Christ speaks to us as never a man spoke. He should be listened to as He speaks to the present day Church.

Chapter Two

Jesus Christ Speaks To Ephesus

SOME OF GOD'S PEOPLE assume in their investigation of the Bible that if a specific book or segment of a book is prophetic, the main message they will discover there needs to do with actualities concerning what's to come. Such isn't the situation, in any case, for Paul lets us know in II Timothy 3:16,17 KJV: "All Scripture is given by inspiration of God, and is profitable for doctrine, for reproof, for correction, for instruction in righteousness: That the man of God might be perfect, thoroughly unto every good work."

An passage of Scripture at that point, might be prophetic, however the message concerning what's to come (future) isn't all that is found in it. God has so built His Word that it brings through all together that His people might be instructed and encouraged, their lives made purer, and their ministry more compelling, more effective by the everlasting, spiritual standards found in His Word.

The letters to the seven churches found in the second and third chapters in the Book of the Revelation are an a valid example. These might be considered from a few distinct perspectives.

Most importantly, they were nearby chronicled houses of worship (local historical churches) in the day when John, under the inspiration of the Holy Spirit, composed the Book of the Revelation. The conditions depicted and the reprobations offered identified with those local circumstances toward the end of the Apostolic age.

Besides, there is likewise in these seven letters an overview of church history from apostolic occasions through to the rapture of the Church.

Thirdly, displayed in these letters are standards by which houses of worship (churches) may assess their actual worth in seeing God at any period amid this church age.

Fourthly, and this is the region of emphasis which will be given in these studies, there is the individual message from Christ to every one of God's children in the Church today. This incorporates warnings and exhortations and promises intended to make the child of God what he ought to be, both as to his own life and to the quality of service he should render.

Dr. John Thomas Wylie

"Unto the heavenly angel of the church of Ephesus write; These things saith he that holdeth the seven stars in his right hand, who walketh amidst the seven golden candlesticks;

I know thy works, and thy labor, and thy patience, and how thou canst not tolerate them which are evil: and thou hast attempted them which say they are messengers (apostles), and are not, and hast discovered them liars; And hast borne, and hast persistence, and for the well-being of my name hast toiled, and hast not fainted.

Nevertheless, I have to somewhat against thee; on the because thou hast left they first love. Keep in mind in this manner from whence thou art fallen, and repent, and do the first works; or else I will come unto thee quickly, and will remove thy candle out of his place, with the except thou repent. In any case, this thou hast that thou hatest the deeds of the Nicolaitanes, which I also despise (hate) (Nicolaitanes is a first century unorthodox group denounced by Jesus in Rev. 2:6,15. They maintained the lessons of Balaam. They denied God as Creator and polished worshipful admiration and liscentiousness).

He that hath an ear, given him a chance to hear what the Spirit saith unto the houses of worship (churches); To him that overcometh will I provide for eat of the tree of life, which is amidst the heaven of God" (Rev. 2:1-7 KJV).

A Person who holds the seven stars in His right hand and who walks amidst the seven golden candlesticks is depicted in Revelation 1:13 as "one like unto the Son of man, dressed with a garment down to the foot." It is simply the Lord Jesus Christ who above all else tells this church that He knows the nature of their service, and their obedience to the faith.

At that point He discusses the one noteworthy defect in their character: "Nevertheless I have to somewhat against thee, on the grounds that thou hast left thy first love."

This is as a general rule an extremely solid explanation, however "somewhat" dilutes its power. In the event that you take a look at your Bible, be that as it may, you will see that "somewhat" is imprinted in italics, implying that it was not in the first dialect or original language.

The emphasis is in reality an extremely strong statement. If He were speaking these words today we would hear them as the voice of numerous waters or conveyed in a voice like thunder. It

Dr. John Thomas Wylie

would be said in love, however it would be said with a firmness and vigor nobody could mistake.

"Left" Not "Lost"

These in the Ephesian church had "left" their first love. They didn't lose it. They deserted it. This was a deliberate leaving of the first love on their part. This love was not lost by them, and they were not looking for it. They abandoned it, and God advised them to go appropriate back to where they abandoned it, for it was there they would discover it. Moreover, he considered it the "first" love. They had left what ought to have been the preeminent love in their lives.

That love is commitment to Christ. This isn't just a show of religion however a heart dedication to the Savior, an affection which has no idea for self in Romans 5:5 "is shed abroad in our souls by the Holy Ghost." It goes a long ways past dutiful love for which men have a characteristic limit. It isn't just human kinship or enjoying or individual heart feeling. Actually, it isn't feeling in any way, however something that springs from a feeling of significant worth put on that which one cherishes.

It's anything but a narrow minded want, however an affection that exhausts itself for individual loved. God so loved the world that He gave Jesus, His beloved Son, so whoever has faith in Him, ought not die but rather ought to have everlasting life.

This love is shown again Philippians chapter two, beginning with verse five: "Continue cultivating a similar mien that Jesus Christ had. Despite the fact that He was existing in the idea of God, He didn't think His being on a uniformity with God a thing to be childishly gotten a handle on, yet He laid it aside as He went up against the idea of a slave and became like other men.

Since He was recognized as a man, truly and in addition in outward form. He at long last humiliated Himself in obedience so as to die, even to die on a cross" (Williams, C. B. 1972). This is the love we are speaking about, a love that originates from God, a love man can not produce.

As we have just observed, it is an love that has been shed abroad in our souls by the Holy Spirit. There is no requirement for the Christian to ask how he may get that love, for he as of now has it. This love, notwithstanding, need to be discharged; and as indicated by I Thessalonians

3:12 KJV, the Lord will increase it in the event that we want a greater amount of it. He will work in and through us to create this love.

As we learn to wait on Him and meditate in His precious Word, this love will grow, and its self-denying characteristics will be more in proof as the days pass by.

It is a quality of love hard to dissect however wonderful in its expression, since the love drew salvation's plan. It is love with singleness of rationale, and a love that sees, as no one but God can see, an incentive, a value in people who are unlovable by human standards.

What is Christ to you? Only your Savior from Sin? Is it accurate to say that he is the One who is setting up a home for you, giving a free ticket to paradise and a confirmation approach against the lake of fire? Or then again would He say He is more than that? Is it true that He is your all? It is safe to say that he is your life?

Think about a home for a minute. What establishes a home? What does a family mean to a man? What does a spouse mean? Is it true that she is one who simply cooks and washes the garments and keeps a clean house? Or then again would she say she is more than that? Is it accurate to say that she is not one who cherishes and is loved in kind? Regardless of whether we live in a little house or a chateau does not make a difference so much only so there is genuine love in the home.

What does Jesus Christ intend to us today? Do we have that strong, firm, imply love for Him? Or on the other hand have we left that first love? It is anything but difficult to end up involved with past achievements, present works, and feasible arrangements more than with Jesus Christ. That is the thing that occurred at Ephesus. Service displaced the Son. The works of Christians were exceptional, and they showed striking persistence under trial; all things considered, their program had jeopardized their spiritual power.

Their Christian activity uprooted, displaced their spiritual fellowship. They were particularly similar to Martha who turned out to be so possessed with serving Jesus that she overlooked the genuine article, that sitting at His feet and taking in His truth.

The record is found in the tenth chapter of Luke beginning with verse 38: "Now as they were journeying on, He went to a specific town where a lady named Martha invited Him to her home. She had a sister named Mary who sat down at the Lord's feet, and remained listening to His message.

In any case, Martha was getting stressed over looking out for them so much, so she came up all of a sudden and stated, "Lord, do you not care that my sister has abandoned me to do all the housework alone? Then tell her to grab hold and help me."

"The Lord addressed her, 'Martha, Martha, you are stressed and vexed over things. Be that as it may, there is real need of couple of things, truly of just a single thing. For Mary has chosen the good portion which must not be taken away from her" (vv. 38-42, Williams Translation, 1972).

Spiritual pride will displace spiritual life. There had never been a real servant of God who withdrew from the faith and has gone into radicalism without first having left his private reverential life and having severed fellowship with the Lord Jesus Christ.

Christian activity that denies one of individual partnership, ransacks that one of usefulness. In this manner Christian activity can turn into a weapon in the hand of Satan. Our service should grow out of our love; only in that way can we avoid this danger.

A Test Of Love

Keep in mind our Savior said to us, "If you love me you will keep my commandments." He didn't state we should keep them, or that we should keep them, but commanded that we really love Him we would keep them.

We demonstrate how little love we have for God when we would tune in to what men say in regards to God than tune in to what God needs to say in regards to Himself. This was valid as far as Israel can tell. They came to Moses and said to him in such a large number of words, "Don't give God a chance to address us. You address us, Moses." They contemplated that if God addressed them possibly they would need to do as He directed or something would transpire. In any case, in the event that it were a man who addressed them, they could before long calm their inner voice concerning what he said.

There is no getting away from the way that we indicate how we love Him by our regard or insolence for what He says. Love was a convincing thing to Paul. It constrained him.

Our Savior stated, "Aside from ye loathe your sibling and sister, and father and mother you can't be my disciple." Does such a strong Scripture entry mean anything to us? If we love Him, it will. We will look through the Scriptures to perceive what is implied by such an irregular explanation. We will discover as we look through that "hate" does not signify "to be angry with," but rather that we love our relatives short of what we love Christ.

Without Him being in the lead position in our hearts, we can't be His followers.

A large number of us who discuss being His disciples don't pursue His teaching. It is suspicious that we even hear him out to hear what He needs to say to us. In any case, when we don't, it is an indication that we don't love Him.

What frustrates us from hearing? Much of the time today the reason lies in the way that we are taken up with such huge numbers of things. We are more worried about how we will live, what kind of vehicle we will drive, where we will go for our entertainment periods, or what we will decide for our dinners, as opposed to putting Christ first. It is conceivable to end up so devoted to things, and to benefit, and even to our feelings that we don't hear what God needs to said to us.

We have to return to where Samuel was when, as a child, he stated, "Speak, Lord, for thy servant heareth."

A Striking Comparison

There is a striking correlation between the congregation at Thessalonica and the congregation at Ephesus. In chapter one of I Thessalonians Paul wrote that he knew about their "work of faith" and "work of labor of love" and "patience of hope." But John in keeping in touch with this church in Ephesus says of them, "I know your works, your labor, and your patience." What a distinction! When your first love is gone all that is left is works, but not works of faith.

When the first love is gone labor progresses toward becoming toil or drudgery. When the first love is gone there is patience but no genuine hope; it is simply a question of endurance. The externalities of work and labor and patience are still there, however the faith which produces works is missing. Love which propels labor is missing with the goal that it turns out to be hard drudge. Hope which produces patience is gone and simple endurance remains.

We should peruse the thirteenth chapter of I Corinthians making this inquiry: "Do I still love Jesus? The outward appearance may state a certain something, however deep down there might be an absence of genuine spiritual life. There are some who have an enthusiasm, zeal for universality which is extremely strange. For confirmation of this read carefully the third chapter of Romans.

Others again may contend for the faith so as to struggle with the life of faith. There might be an enthusiasm for reprimand (denunciation) of sin and for the proclamation of truth, however it is a zeal that isn't persuaded by love.

At the point when love is missing, it is easy for hate to assume control. Keep in mind how Jeremiah, the weeping prophet, loved God and God's people, Israel. We would do well to seek to pattern our love after his.

We read in I John 2:15 ASV that we are to "love not the world." Here again the word for love conveys the significance of putting a high value on something.

For this situation we are advised on what we are not to place a high value. We are not to love the things of the world. When we completely comply with this Scripture, matters around us won't disturbed us. In the event that we put Jesus Christ first, there is nothing around us that will pulverize the internal peacefulness of our lives.

If we are slanted to get agitated with things or individuals, this standard will turn out to be a decent test for us. When we figure individuals don't comprehend us, or in the event that we are in the ministry and we figure Christians don't value our sermons, it is exceptionally conceivable that we have put too high an incentive on the wrong things rather than on Jesus Christ.

The Remedy

Not exclusively did our Lord tell the church at Ephesus what their basic spiritual issue was, but He additionally demonstrated to them how to remedy it. They had left their first love, now how might they come back to it? The arrangement is given in these words: "Remember therefore from whence thou art fallen, and repent, and do the first works" (v. 5). The cure displayed here is threefold, and we should be mindful so as not to give this word from God make no more impression on us than water running off a duck's back, for then we will be faced with genuine trouble for sure.

Dr. John Thomas Wylie

Above all else, we are approached to "remember." The prodigal son had to reach the finish of himself before he remembered. It was the point at which he was sitting in the hog pen eating with the swines, cool conceivably, and sick clad with no spot in that nation to call home, he begun to act normally again and remembered his father's home. What's more, we know from the anecdote that his father was all the while sitting tight for him.

The prodigal son could have remembered sooner, however he didn't. Let us not hold up so long that He needs to bring us totally as far as possible to the end of ourselves before we remember.

The following word to note is "repent." It means to turn back first in the heart and after that in purpose. We are to turn back to the love we have left. We abandoned (left it) it some place, the inquiry; where is the place? The prodigal son had left his first love at home. He went to the far country loving himself. It might require us a little investment to beware of our own spiritual condition, but if we are careful before God and sincerely look through our hearts, He will demonstrate to us where we left that first love.

Then there follows the about face. The reckless (prodigal son) stated, "I will arise and go," as well as he got up and went home. Repentance isn't something in words only, it isn't simply merely intention - it incorporates activity. It isn't only, "I will," but, "I do."

We may well ask the question, Why do I serve God today? Some may reply, "I have been chosen to my to play out a specific service for the Lord." Another may state, "I have a specific blessing and that blessing is helpful in the Lord's service." So far as God is concerned, these are not basic reason or purposes behind our serving Him. They might be miscellaneous items en route, but there is just a single genuine purpose behind obvious support of God, one that He embraces. It is our love for Him and for a lost world, a love for souls that God loved and gave His Son for.

The third word is recommended by the phrase, "And do the first works." This implies something must be repeated. The first works are the result of the first love. This love will be repeated in our hearts just as we steadily look for it. What's more, there is just a single place to discover it - appropriate here in His own love letters to us - the

Bible, and by spiritual correspondence with Him based on what He has uncovered to us.

Israel's involvement regarding the manna in the wilderness represents this reality for us generally plainly. The Israelites needed to go out every morning before the sun came up and liquefied the nourishment, and assemble enough for one day. On account of the Israelites, obviously, this precious food was for their physical bodies, however it has a spiritual or typical significance for us.

Every one needed to assemble for himself. That is how it is in the spiritual domain (realm).

We won't be restored to our first love by tuning in to better messages, setting off to a superior church, or deciding to improve the situation later on.

We will think that its just as we get alone with God and admit to Him that we have left that love some place, but we need it restore it once more. We need to put Jesus Christ first in our hearts.

Be straightforward with God in this. There is nothing we can hide from Him regardless, however it is fundamental for us to be completely forthright and open before Him as we admit these issues. At that point we can put ourselves at His disposal so that by and by He will able to love through us. All things considered, this love with which we are managing isn't a man-made love. It isn't normal to man by any stretch of the imagination. It's anything but a love for sentiment or believing or of insignificant human empathy in any form. It far rises above human love.

A Warning

Following the announcement of the remedy is this warning: "Else I will come unto thee rapidly, and will evacuate thy candle out of his place, with the exception of thou repent." The happening to the Lord spoken here isn't His second coming.

What is implied is an individual, administered judgment, one not lefty to other people, but rather something the Lord should do Himself to take the diciple back to his unique walk with Him.

The strategy He utilizes is to evacuate the lampstand. Presently this lampstand isn't a candle however a candle holder. Every neighborhood church was to be a light revealer. Every assemblage held up the light, which is Jesus Christ. So the warning is that Christ will evacuate what holds up the light except if there is contrition. He won't permit those to be light bearers who are not themselves hearing a good testimony to Him.

The Holy Spirit has been sent to us all together that through us, He may present Jesus Christ to the world. It is only the power and the life of the Spirit inside us that empowers us to lift up Christ, the Light. What is meant here, at that point, is that the Spirit of God will leave the unrepentant believers to a weak observer for Christ. He won't abandon them so far as salvation is concerned, but their ability to present Christ as He truly is will be no more. The power for seeing will be expelled.

Jesus Christ has sent the Holy Spirit, and the Holy Spirit endued certain men with spiritual endowments.

At that point these gifted men were given to the church by Christ. Through the Spirit, these Spirit-filled men in the church witness to the living Christ and in this sense are the lampstand. At the point when the lampstand is expelled, the association all things considered may proceed, but it will be without a nurturing declaration.

The request of that expulsion is seen here too. To start with, the activity of the Spirit through that specific church will stop. This will likewise apply to the people in the congregation. The skilled men God has given to the congregation, men who remain Spirit-filled, will be expelled. The association, as we have stated, will remain, but their capacity for witnessing will be no more.

Much activity might be in proof however no genuine convicting message. At first this expulsion will be unnoticed by the greater part of the people included. What's more, with the dynamic work of the Holy Spirit missing from their midst the ability to discern spiritual things will likewise be gone. There will be no genuine information of the way that spiritual power has abandoned them.

In sight of God, there will be no more a get together of disciples to that place, just a gathering of religious individuals. With the love for Christ gone, the light will be no more. What remains will be simply sounding brass, void declaration, unimportant religion, action of no value.

We can apply this to ourselves and to the churches with which we are associated. We can glance around and see Christian schools and even mission social orders and perceive how they remain in connection to the issue. Is the real witness gone? Is there a social good news of the genuine gospel? Is everything movement with no power? Say thanks to God for those in whom the true light is as yet shining?

This is a genuine issue. We should hearken to the voice of God. This warning should make us work for the Lord in fear and trembling (Phil. 2:12). What a catastrophe it is have God expel the lampstand from any of us, either as people or with respect to the organizations through which we serve!

Chapter Three

Jesus Christ Speaks To Smyrna

THIS WAS A NEARBY church which endured incredible persecution. It likewise speaks to in the prophetic picture that period of the Church's history while amid the early hundreds of years, especially the second and third, there was wave after influx of persecution. A few Christians may not understand it, but rather in the last couple of ages in our day a portion of the most exceedingly terrible oppressions and persecutions against the Church of Jesus Christ have been endured in different lands.

The end isn't yet, and we are reminded that they who live Godly in Christ Jesus will suffer persecution. The standards set down here are guides for us today, demonstrating what the disposition of the Christian ought to be when persecution comes.

"And unto the angel of the church in Smyrna write; These things saith the first and the last, which was dead, and is alive; I know thy works, and tribulation, and poverty, (but thou art rich) and I know the blasphemy of them which say they are Jews, and are not, but rather are the synagogue of Satan.

Fear none of these things which thou shalt suffer: Behold, the devil shall cast some of you into prison, that ye might be tried; and ye will shall have tribulation ten days; be thou faithful unto death, and I will give thee a crown of life. He that hath an ear, let him hear what the Spirit saith unto the churches; He that overcometh shall not be hurt of the second death" (Rev. 2:8-11 KJV).

The Lord Jesus presents Himself as "the First and the Last." This is both revealing and comforting to a church suffering opposition, or to a christian under serious trial. When every one of the persecutors are gone, the One who is the First and the Last will still be with us. In addition, the persecutors should stand before Him and answer for their evil deeds.

There is a phase of persecution today that ought to never be. It is a persecution of Christians by Christians in which the most disgraceful, shameful kind of character assassination often takes place. Today, is a day of simple, easy, far reaching correspondence with the goal that the chances to spread a man's character and to spread that smear far and wide is straightforward compared with what it was a few years ago.

Regularly the main explanation behind such assaults by one Christian against another can be followed to insufficient information. One believer does not comprehend what work another is trying to do or plainly recognize what standards he is following. It might even be that the critical party does not approve of the places to which the other goes, or the kind of people to whom he preaches.

We apparently have overlooked that God's people are His servants and they must answer as people to Him. We have no privilege, no right to defame or to attack someone else's servant. We, as well, must give account for things we do with regard to God's children. The majority of this will turn out at the judgment Seat of Christ to the extent Christians are concerned.

Our Lord is likewise portrayed as the One who was dead and is alive. He too was persecuted, even unto death, but He arose again from the grave. He has boundless, unlimited authority to manage the persecutors and to vindicate the persecuted. He suffered a horrible death, upon the cross where He assumed our guilt.

Be though He died, He also rose again, which brings incredible assurance for all who are persecuted. Because He lives His people will live also. We may lose our real lives, we may likewise lose all our property, all that we have in this world, but we can't lose Him. Nothing can isolate us from the love for God which is in Christ Jesus, our Lord.

There is no judgment recorded against this church. This in itself is a commendation without need of elaboration regarding the matter. God's silence or seeming silence, that we suffer long, does not imply that He isn't concerned. It might be the proof of His endorsement, and we by faith acknowledge it as such. If it is important for Him to make a lot over us, applaud us, convey us along, and feed us some calming elixir constantly, it could be an indication that we are not living under persecution in the way in which He wants us to live.

Three Things

There are three things in this segment Christ says He knows. He is the All-knowing One, who sees the end from the beginning. Nothing ever escapes Him. He says here as a result: "I know your tribulation; I know your poverty; and I know the blasphemy of specific ones who guarantee to be something they are most certainly not."

The word deciphered "tribulation" in this entry fits the portrayal of a portion of the persecution we find in our day under Godless, skeptical, atheistic governments. Men have been tormented to death in inhumane imprisonments by a wide range of means and techniques - the most frightful that could be brainstormed.

The word for tribulation is a solid one, discussing incredible pressure instead of little tests of faith. Conceivably a decent outline of the word would be found in the old flour plants which utilized stones to granulate the grain until the point when it is pulverized fine (a few years prior). Such is the sort of abuse discussed here.

Jesus was crushed that way. He said "I am not a man, I resemble a worm that has been crushed" (Ps. 22). The majority of us have never suffered to this degree. also, we may never do as such. Notwithstanding, if times proceed as they may be, this could be the part of a significant number of us, except if our Savior comes and takes the Church home to be with Himself.

Point of fact, the entire world will see things it has never seen before in the domain of persecution and scorn as the basis for the Antichrist and his malevolent, evil rule is laid. We have countless numbers of the Antichrist today, men who, however not simply the real person himself, have huge numbers of his qualities, especially their disdain against the Christian and Christ.

The Lord additionally says here, "I know thy poverty." The word truly signifies "beggary." They had endured the loss of all things. this is a similar word that depicts our Savior who was rich and ended up poor, as per II Corinthians 8:9. Exactly how poor did He move toward becoming? He exited the wonders of paradise with it hordes of holy messengers (angels) serving Him and came to earth where He had nearly nothing or little.

He shared our poverty that through His riches we may be made rich. This was His message to Smyrna, and it is the equivalent to us, today, for the present Church.

In the third place, He knew the individuals who were of the synagogue of Satan, who professed to be Jews however were most certainly not. What's more, there are many like them today. Some claim to be the one hundred and forty-four thousand. Others guarantee that their congregation association is the only true church. Except if a man joins their specific gathering he can not be saved. God arranges all, for example, the "synagogue of Satan." That is certifiably not a satisfying grouping to make, however it is one God has made, not us.

A Word Of Comfort

Presently an expression of comfort is given. Those at Smyrna were advised to "fear none of those things" which they would suffer. There are adherents who endure in light of the fact that they are Christians and not on the grounds that they have done anything incorrectly. This, obviously, is evidence of the honest nature of their character.

Here again we should be wary, on guard. In most unforeseen methods for our adversary can trip us up. To feel frustrated about ourselves could be an allurement when aggrieved. We may well inquire as to whether we are being developed in the Word today so that if languishing over the faith should come our direction we would have the capacity to stand up under it, cheer in it, and not be loaded up with self-pity.

Take our Savior for an example. He suffered without opening His mouth in objection or even to shield, or defend Himself. he was driven as a sheep to the butcher and as a sheep, idiotic before its shearers, He opened not His mouth. He didn't look to vindicate Himself. There are authentic men today who have been insulted and assaulted however have declined to vindicate themselves, abandoning it to God to do it for them.

Moses was a meek man, conceivably the meekest who at any point lived, as per the Scriptures, but he suffered. One reason he is called meek is that he didn't protect himself when extremely condemned. The facts confirm that toward an incredible finish he spoke a few words in an attack of outrage that brought discipline upon him. He was not allowed to enter the Promised Land.

Furthermore, the reason God made such a model for Moses' situation was because of his position. The fundamental point, in any case, is that Moses experienced criticism and persecution from men, especially from his very own country and family, but he didn't try to vindicate himself. He allowed God to take care of that.

Dr. John Thomas Wylie

Attitude In Trials

The admonition God provided for the church of Smyrna was, "Fear none of these things." He didn't promise them relief. Truth be told, there was the possibility of further oppression and persecution in front of them.

This is in opposition to what individuals today figure God ought to do. Some of them are stating, "If God is a God of love for what reason doesn't He stop such persecution?" There is a valid justification why God permits it, for out of persecution comes the genuine individual. If we as Christians live faithful in Christ Jesus, we will suffer persecution (II Tim. 3:12 ASV). Why? All together that we may know Christ better and be more similar to Him.

Job suffered incredible hardships and persecution on account of Satan. In any case, toward the finish of his sufferings Job could state, "I have known about thee by the becoming aware of the ear; however now mine eye seeth thee. Wherefore I severely dislike myself, and repent in residue and fiery debris." And in somewhere else he stated, "When he hath tried me, I will come forth as gold."

There are different segments of Scripture which reveal to us what our state of mind ought to be towards trials. Peter wrote, "Rejoice, in light of the fact that ye are partakers of Christ's sufferings; that, when his glory will be uncovered, ye might be glad also with exceeding joy" (I Pet. 4:13). We are not to be down and out under oppression or persecution, but rather to rejoice, in light of the fact that thee will be added glory for us in the day when Christ shows up.

Again Peter lets us know: "If ye be rebuked for the name of Christ, happy are ye; for the spirit of glory and of God resteth upon you; on their part he is evil spoken of, but on your part he is glorified" (I Pet. 4:14 KJV). There is no compelling reason to feel ashamed but instead to rejoice when faced with such conditions.

An expression of caution or warning pursues these admonitions. Peter says, "But let none of you suffer as a murderer, or as a thief, or as a evildoer, or as a meddler in other men's issues. However on the off chance that any man suffer as a Christian, let him not be ashamed; but let him glorify God on this behalf." The day is coming when God will glorify His name through us in a way that we have no understanding of up 'til now.

Dr. John Thomas Wylie

In the last verse of this fourth chapter, Peter expresses: "Wherefore let them that suffer according to the will of God commit the keeping of their souls to him in well doing, as unto a faithful Creator."

Our God is loyal, faithful and when we are persuaded of this we will never address what He allows us to go through.

He is in every case right; this we should remember and be settled upon. He comprehends what He is doing and has promised that in the event that we are faithful, He will give us the crown of life. This isn't eternal life for we gotten that the minute we confided in Christ. It is something added to the believer's salvation. A crown talks about sovereignty and of triumph.

We will be more than champions through Him. the person who defeats will not be harmed of the second death. What an extraordinary confirmation this is for the holy person, but what an incredible affirmation this is for the holy person, but what a grave cautioning and judgment for one who does not know Jesus Christ as Savior.

Chapter Four

Jesus Christ Speaks To Pergamos

"AND TO THE ANGEL of the church in Pergamos write: These things saith he which hath the sharp sword with two edges; I know thy works, and where thou dwellest, even where Satan's seat is: and holdest quick my name, and hast not denied my faith, even in those days wherein Antipas was my faithful martyr, who was killed among you, where Satan dwelleth.

"But I have a few of things against thee, in light of the fact that thou hast there them that hold the doctrine of Balaam, who encouraged Balac to cast a stumbling block before the children of of Israel, to eat things sacrificed unto idols, and to commit fornication.

So hast thou also them that hold the doctrine of the Nicolaitanes, which thing I hate. Repent; or else I will come unto thee quickly, and will fight against them with the sword of my mouth.

"He that hath an ear, let him hear what the Spirit saith unto the churches; To him that over cometh will I give to eat of the hidden manna, and will give him a white stone, and in the stone a new name written, which no man knoweth saving he that receiveth it" (Rev. 2:1`2-17 KJV).

The church of Pergamos was situated in an extraordinary center of idol worship. The idolatry practiced in that area was to a great extent the worship of nature. Exceptional among the animals loved was the snake. This may help clarify a portion of the references in the letter.

The Saviour portrays Himself here as the One who has the sharp sword with two edges. This is an image talking about insight and official power. As indicated by the first chapter of the Book of the Revelation the sword was not in His grasp but rather in His mouth. Therefore it needs to do with His Word - as opposed to execution.

Christ words to Pergamos were: "I know thy works, and where thou dwellest." God knew where they lived and He knows where we live. Today, we are living in a universe of riches and design. Mammon has become our God. Our emphasis is upon the material things of life instead of the spiritual. It would appear just as a significant number of us serve God just when it

Dr. John Thomas Wylie

is convenient. This is true even of many who are in full-time service for the Lord.

Here in the United States we have what we call separation of church and state (we ought to have cooperation of church and state). We have no state church. As indicated by this standard, the church can't dictate to the government neither can the government dictate to the church. Then again, genuine Christianity ought to pervade our administration through the men who serve in it.

In any case, we find that today the doctrine of the separation of church and state has come to intend to some that Christianity is to be kept out of everything aside from the church. Our schools, which were once established on christian standards, are increasingly notwithstanding the Bible. Our government, which likewise was established in a substantial measure on Christian standards, is endeavoring to make an unnatural separation between Christian thought and government.

Separation of church and state does not imply that Christ ought to have no place in the lives of our people in government and that His principles should not direct them in their choices. At the point when there was regard in all components of our general public for the Word of God and the conviction was general that Jesus Christ was the everlasting Son of God, there was an alternate climate in the nation. In any case, that is all evolving quick. Satan is prevailing upon, and the Bible is being kept out of our public life wherever possible.

Power To Convict And To Convert

We also observe that this One who has the sword leaving His mouth has, through His Word and His Spirit, the ability to convict and furthermore to convert. This is the reason we are to preach the Word.

This same Word will likewise condemn a man. If you who read this don't have Jesus Christ as your own Savior, the Word of God will convict you of this disregard (neglect) if you will read it; or-and this an interesting point - it will condemn you whether you read it or not.

The Word of God is portrayed as a sword in Hebrews 4:12,13 KJV where we read: "For the Word of God is quick" (living and operative). It is unique in relation to some other word. I may peruse some incredible writer like Shakespeare or some other common essayist, and I may appreciate what I read or I may reject what I read, but such perusing is completely not quite the same as that of the Word of God itself.

That Word implied something to my spirit when I was a youthful Christian, an angel (babe) in Christ. Today that same Word is as still living and working in me in a more significant manner than any time in recent memory. It has the power to divide asunder soul and spirit.

The Word of God unmistakably distinguishes the soulish life and the spiritual life. The soul has to do basically with life in the substance (flesh), while the spirit has to do with that which concerns God. At the point when Christ comes into our hearts, He takes up His position in the spirit of man and from that point He starts to control the soul and the body.

All three of them are spoken to here in the Word of God. Nothing is avoided the seeking of that Word. It passes judgment on the thoughts and the intents of the heart. No creature can avoid Him. Everything is naked and open unto the eyes of Him with whom we have to do. The Word of God enters the heart as nothing else will, that is the reason we should preach the Word.

Cults of the present day take a little piece of the Word here and a little there, utilizing just what they need and leave the rest. By this technique they have developed numerous false frameworks and principles and have even brought division among believers as a result.

Satan's Throne

Another factor to consider here is that God knows where we abide as well as realizes where Satan's position of authority is. It would show up from this that there are sure areas or regions where Satan will set up himself, in any event for a period. It is obvious at that point, that Christians in such places will be under more noteworthy stress, anxiety from Satanic assault than maybe some others more distant expelled from Satan's primary place of operation.

This leads us to this further idea: a few of us are presented to impulses to which others are definitely not. There are allurements of sin around some that are not around others. Hence, if any of us will pass judgment on the character of another Christian brother, we ought to make certain we know where he lives in the Bible significance of that term.

In all actuality, since we may not know where someone in particular lives in regard to these things we have been dealing with, it is best for us not to pass judgment on his character too extremely. God says, "I know the intents and purposes of your heart. I know your heart motives. I know under what conditions you have to work."

The Apostle Paul in keeping in writing to the Corinthians, communicated this issue in clear terms. he stated, "As for me, myself, it is of almost no worry to me to be analyzed by you or any human court; actually, I don't even examine myself. For in spite of the fact that my inner voice does not charge me, yet I am not by any means vindicated by that. It is simply the Lord who must look at me.

So you should quit forming any untimely judgments, but hold up until the point that the Lord will come back once more; for He will uncover the insider facts covered up in obscurity and will make known the thought processes of men's hearts, and the best possible praise will be granted each of us" (I Cor. 4:3-5 KJV), (Williams Translation, 1972).

The fifth verse is very important in this matter of making a decision about judging motives. Paul is stating as a result that the Corinthians did not know the thought processes back of his activities; in this manner, it was unrealistic for them to form right conclusions regarding his overall service.

It is so natural to scrutinize brutally a kindred Christian when he falls. What's more, we do this so promptly despite the fact that we don't recognize what was in the individual's heart, and know minimal about the circumstances paving the way to the fall. It is a lot less demanding to carry on with a genuine life under a few circumstances than it is under some others. It will take the omniscient Christ to decide the credit or fault due any of us.

We would need to know how much a person needed to resist before we could properly pass judgment on his character. We would likewise need to know how simple or troublesome it may be for somebody to run the race. A few people, as we have stated, don't have issues that others have. So in the light of these certainties, given us a chance to be cautious in our estimations of other individuals' lives.

We may judge cruelly for a situation where the Savior would not do as such since He is all-knowing. We may, then again, compliment

Dr. John Thomas Wylie

someone else when as a general rule there is nothing that our Savior would commend him for.

This does not imply that we are not to indicate wisdom concerning what individuals may do. The Savior has given another guideline, to be specific that by their fruits we will know certain ones. It is one thing to perceive an activity with respect to a Christian as being off-base (being wrong), it is very another for us to sit as judge, expecting the right that has a place only with Christ.

This does not mean we will overlook sin and not condemn it, but rather it means we will be exceptionally limited in our treatment of the guilty party, and utilize incredible caution in attributing motives to him. The exhortation by Paul in Galatians 6 to restore one who falls' is to the individuals who are spiritual, and they are to be mindful so as to consider the way that they themselves are inclined to fall into a similar sort of transgression (sin).

Circumstances under which we work may all be on surface, simple for all to see. Then again, they might be felt only in the internal recesses of a person's heart, and no one but God can know that. Also, let us not imagine that since somebody can confront the world and his kindred believers with a joyful testimony and let that joy be reflected in the happiness of his face that he is without trials. He has them, but has conceivably figured out how to rejoice in the Lord despite them.

We can thank God that at the Judgment Seat of Christ every one of these issues or matters will be made plain. Furthermore, some who have been highly praised here on earth may not be so highly praised there. Some who are first here might be last there.

Satan has his position of authority, his base of tasks, his base camp at better places at various occasions. He isn't omnipresent like God. Since he is a angelic being, be that as it may, Satan is able to move rapidly starting with one area then onto the next, yet he isn't all-powerful and all-knowing. Thus far as the Christian is concerned, he is to remember that Satan is a crushed enemy, a defeated foe. His power is past that of any of us as people, however it isn't past that of any of us who walk in the power of the Holy Spirit (See James 4:7 KJV).

Satan's kingdom is obviously efficient. Daniel at one time had the response to one of his prayers deferred due to the activity of one of Satan's prince leaders. Be that as it may, in the long run the message from God reached the prophet disregarding all that Satan and his companions could do.

Satan utilizes different strategies, contingent upon the conditions he discovers Christians in. At Smyrna he set up a "synagogue" contradicting the work of the Lord through a religious framework.

At Pergamos he utilized persecution even unto death against believers. God knows every one of these things and all else beside, so we can certainly rest our faith in him who is our faithful Creator and Redeemer. He knows as nobody else does whether our service is in the power of the Spirit or in the flesh.

A Difference In Methods

God's method is to work through the spirit of man, while Satan approaches him from the stance of his soulish life. Satan begins all things considered and attempts to work in, however God begins from within and works out.

The Word of God depicts itself as being "more keen than any two-edged sword, puncturing even to the isolating apart of soul and spirit." A large number individuals have never taken in this distinction, but it is an indispensable one. We read in Philippians that the believer is to work out his own salvation with fear and trembling. The significance of the passage, to the extent I can comprehend it, is that God comes in and claims the internal center of man's being, the soul, and tenets his life both soul and body from that source.

We discuss the body having five senses, specifically sight, hearing, smell, taste, and touch. Undoubtedly there are properties in the soul, for example, conscience, emotion, mentality, will, and consciousness. These would all be able to react either to Satan or to God.

So capable is the adversary that he can trick us into supposing we are really being honored of God in our very own hearts when as a general rule we are doing just reacting on an absolutely human dimension to specific things that intrigue and satisfy us.

For instance given us a chance to state that we go to a melodic show. The music is magnificent, and the words appear to contain a message for us. We tune in and end up lifted ever more elevated in our enthusiastic reaction. at that point, after

Dr. John Thomas Wylie

the show is over we leave the place saying, "What a gift, a blessing I got from that music."

There may have been something there that may have made us think truly on some part of life, yet maybe one of our friends downplayed it and we all together dismissed it. We went home, still keen to the music, yet there was nothing in the experience that drove us to our knees. There was nothing in the show that truly conveyed us up close and personal with a choice that must be made for the Lord.

Music, obviously, may not be capable in itself to bring us to such a place; but then again, there are the individuals who trust that since they have been sincerely blended they have been conveyed nearer to God through such means. Now that is a genuine slip-up. Soulish response isn't the equivalent as a spiritual response.

Over against such an ordeal as has quite recently been portrayed we may have heard a message which drove home truth to our souls so when we went home we needed to go to a private place and get alone with the Lord.

Exactly what is the distinction between the two? One has just joined itself to our feelings and made us feel better. However, the impression left on us went poorly our emotions; though the message with its spiritual power got down into the spiritual piece of our being, and we settled things with God. This is the consequence of Christ having complete control of the spirit which thus impacts the soul and this impact is communicated in and through the body.

Then again, when we begin with the body at that point go to the soul, we turned out to be egotistical. Our entire life is revolved around our own advantages. We ask ourselves, "What am I getting out of this? Am I going to be lifted up?" Our considerations are dependably on self for a situation like that.

Holding His Name

Various commendations are given the church of Pergamos, the first of these is, "thou holdest quick my name." The name for this situation has to do with the person of Jesus Christ. An unbeliever may utilize the name of our Lord wrongly. Others may utilize the name of Jesus and discuss Him as an extraordinary educator and an incredible precedent but at the same time miss the mark regarding holding quick His name.

He is the Great God, the First and the Last, the One who made all things. The unscriptural encouraging that Jesus Christ was the first made being is an old one and has gone up against new power in the present day. The Bible does not teach that Jesus was simply the first made being, however that He Himself is endless, eternal and is the Creator of all things.

There is an extraordinary puzzle and furthermore incredible wonders regarding the coming of the Lord Jesus Christ into this world as the Babe of Bethlehem. The supernatural occurrence of the virgin birth was cultivated through the power of the Holy Spirit.

Furthermore, that reality that the eternal God came as an individual is one of the remarkable tests utilized regarding an instructor or a prophet, demonstrating whether he is true or false. John wrote in his general epistle: "Beloveth, believe few not every spirit, but try the spirits whether they are of God; because many false prophets are gone out into the world.

Hereby know ye the Spirit of God: Every soul that confesseth that Jesus Christ is come in the flesh is of God: And every soul that confesseth not that Jesus Christ is come in the flesh is not of

God; and this is that spirit of antichrist, whereof ye have heard that it should come; and even now already is it in the world" (I John 4:1-3).

I Corinthians 12:3 KJV says, that a man can't state that Jesus is the eternal God with the exception of as that one is lit up by the Holy Spirit. Subsequently, the man who accepts and straightforwardly admits with his mouth that Jesus Christ is the interminable God is a genuine educator.

It isn't sufficient for a man to state, "I trust that Jesus is everlastingly God, but I don't talk about it." The genuine righteous man not only trusts it, he admits it, he confesses it. Furthermore, as indicated by the Scripture in I John it isn't necessary for a man to straightforwardly deny that Christ is eternally God with the end goal to be related to the spirit of Antichrist.

The plain truth that he doesn't confess that Jesus Christ is come in the flesh marks him as having a place with the enemy. This other certainty is likewise valid: When a religious educator denies the virgin birth of the Lord Jesus Christ, we realize that instructor isn't of God, but of the spirit of Antichrist. From such we are to dismiss, turn away.

We consider the X-ray device to be a wonderful development and has possessed the capacity to serve healing centers (hospitals) for quite a while. Be that as it may, the amount more noteworthy is the power of God who can tell our thoughts even a far distance off, as the psalmist said. The Lord knows our works, and where we stay, and what we are doing for His Name's sake, and what we are neglecting to do. There is nothing hid from God.

Holding To The Faith

Another commendation given to this congregation is that they had not denied "my faith." This faith isn't something that can be distinguished as "our faith" in the feeling of our denominational belief. Men may talk about their various types of beliefs, but there is just a single genuine, true faith and that is portrayed here by the Lord as "my faith."

This is the faith that we have in Jesus Christ; and as per Galatians 2:20 KJV it is the "faith of the Son of God who loved me and gave Himself for me."

In this association there is a passage which has baffled huge numbers of God's people. It is

Colossians 1:23 where we perused: "If ye proceed in the faith grounded and settled, and be not moved far from the expectation of the gospel, which ye have heard, and which was preached each creature which is under paradise; whereof I Paul am made a minister."

The expression, "if ye continue in the faith, grounded and settled," is the root of the issue. Numerous Christians on perusing this consider how thin the string is on which their salvation hangs. In this expression in its unique situation, and this will assist us with the articulation "my faith" in the Book of the Revelation.

Starting with Colossians 1:21 KJV we have these words: "And you, that were at some point distanced and adversaries in your brain by insidious works, but now hath he accommodated. In the body of his flesh through death, to introduce you holy and unblameable and unreproveable in his sight: If ye proceed in the faith grounded and settled."

There are two unmistakable periods of salvation alluded to here, but the two are so nearly close together that they ought not be isolated in our reasoning. They are not free (independent) of one another, but rather this is the place such a large number of Christians commit mistakes regarding them.

The first subject is our reconciliation to God. Before we were saved, we were enemies, estranged from God, and dead in trespasses and sins. Be that as it may, through His death, Christ removed the punishment and blameworthy (guilt) of our transgression (sin) making it possible for us to be reconciled to God. This is affirmed in Romans 5:10 RSV which understands: "We were reconciled to God by the death of his Son."

That is the first phase of salvation, and we received it by faith. We are saved by grace through faith.

The second phase has to do with our life as believers. We live by His life or as Galatians 2:20 RSV says, we live "by the faith of the Son of God." Our Savior made the promise in the tenth chapter of John that He came not only to give us life, but that we may have it all the more abundantly. The giving of life has to do with our being reconciled to God.

The second part has to do with this same life being communicated through us by the living Christ who lives in us. These, as we have called attention to, are two unmistakable phases of salvation, however the one pursues the other. They are both part of a same life that God gives us when we trust in Jesus Christ.

The purpose of the Lord Jesus, once we are reconciled, is to live through us and to present us holy, unblameable, and unreproveable in His sight.

It is His constant aim in our lives to bring us to maturity. Also, we achieve maturity by the same method for appropriating life as we did when we initially believed. It is a walk of faith. Be that as it may, this is the place such a significant number of commit a grave error. Their reasoning is by all accounts that they are saved at first by faith, but they are kept saved by works.

The Bible teaches us that we are saved by faith and we are kept by faith. In any case, there is more than that in the teaching of the Scripture. We grow to maturity only as we day by day appropriate the fact that Jesus Christ is living in us. If we continue in this faith we will mature to where we can be presented by our Savior holy and unblameable.

Else, we will have to meet Him at the Judgment Seat of Christ where our works will be tried; and if they are simply our works, they will be wood, hay, and stubble and will burn. If they are His, created by His faith in us, they will be gold, silver, valuable stones and will remain.

It is no wonder, then, that we are advised to continue in the faith. We are not to hop from faith for salvation to something unique with the end goal to achieve perfection. "As ye have therefore received Christ Jesus the Lord, so walk ye in him" is Paul's exhortation in Colossians 2:6.

We should not enable anybody to agitate us with the customs of men or vain philosophies, for these will shield us from being built up in the things of Christ.

We are not brought to maturity in the Christian life by keeping the Law of Moses, as some thought in the early church and as some show us even at this point.

The things charged upon us are not given all together that we may continue being Christians; however now that we are Christians they turned into the expression of the living Christ in and through us. He will consequently deliver in us the sort of life that pleases Him.

The reason a few Christians live in a hopeless life is that they have neglected to keep trusting God for their every day victory. That is the reason they lose their tempers and do different things in spite of the new existence of Jesus Christ inside them.

This takes place within us when we don't trust in God for our daily life. After having having finished His atoning work in us, He then proceeds to perfect the new life in us.

The Doctrine Of Balaam

ALL that was said to Pergamos was not by way of commendation. Not all was appropriate among them, and there are several marks against against them.

In any case there were the individuals who held the doctrine of Balaam. The charge was not excessively all individuals from that church clung to this doctrine however there were some in their midst who did. What's more, the way that some did was an unmistakable sign that the others were not practicing church discipline. The church was steadfast, loyal in the faith, but it was tolerating false perspectives.

What is this doctrine of Balaam? We have to know, for it is a sort of teaching that Satan has utilized against the work of God on several occasions.

The authentic foundation or the historical background concerning this doctrine is found in Numbers chapters 22 through 25. There we discover that Balaam was contracted (hired) by Balak, king of Moab, to curse the general population of Israel when they went through the place that is known for Moab on their approach to Canaan. Balak feared them and wanted them destroyed.

He realized his armed forces were not strong enough to carry out the job, so he hired Balaam, a barbarian or heathen diviner, who for some odd reason likewise knew something of the true God, to bring down a curse upon Israel. Balaam attempted to win his ill-gotten wages, but discovered that as opposed to cursing Israel he blessed them. God would not enable this evil prophet to curse the nation God had blessed.

Balaam found that Israel, as a country, was secure in God's hand. This security laid on God's sovereign will, grace and mercy, which was first uncovered to Abraham in Genesis 12. The record is, "I will bless thee, and will make of thee a great nation."

This was an unconditional promise God gave His servant. From one point of view, at that point, Israel was resistant to Satan's assaults.

They were resistant to the adversary's stroke. The final purposes of God in that nation could not be permanently ruined.

But, this is just one side of the issue. We should not stop here or we won't see the awfulness of the wrongdoing (sin) of the doctrine of Balaam.

This is the divine record of what happened when Balaam, rather than cursing Israel, blessed them saying, "How shall I will I curse, whom God hath not cursed? Or how shall I defy, whom the Lord hath not defied? For from the top of the rocks I see him, and from the hills I behold him: lo, the people will dwell alone, and will not be reckoned among the nations" (vv. 8,9).

Again in the same chapter we read, "Rise up, Balak, and hear; hearken unto me, thou son of Zippor: God isn't a man, that he should lie; neither the son of man, that he should repent: hath he said, and will he not do it? or or hath he spoken, and will he not make it good?

Behold, I have received commandment to bless: and he hath blessed; and I can not reverse it. He hath not beheld iniquity in Jacob, neither hath he seen perverseness in Israel; the Lord his God is with him, and the shout of a king is among them" (vv. 18-21).

Dr. John Thomas Wylie

In this fashion God pronounced Israel's situation as a nation before Him and a ultimate purpose He had for them. Balaam and Balak were the emissaries of Satan in this incident, and in dealing with such foes God proclaims His ultimate purpose with regard to His people.

In chapter 24 Balaam emphasizes the fact that he can't curse Israel but should bless them and in the meantime talk against Moab in doing so. The future glory of Israel's place in the kingdoms of the world is found in verse 17: "I shall see him, but not now: I will behold him, but not nigh: there shall come a Star out of Jacob, and a Scepter shall rise out of Israel, and will smite the corners of Moab, and destroy all of the children of Sheth."

This, as we have stated, is one side of the inquiry. This identifies with God's everlasting and sovereign purpose for Israel. He will in the long run set them up in their land, and make them His own people, and put His love and into their hearts.

No adversary can curse them to where this sovereign purpose of God will be permanently thwarted. His promise to Abraham in Genesis 12 will be literally fulfilled.

Over against this, we find that the nation of Israel suffered over its wrongdoings (sins), and people in the nation languished over their transgressions (sins). The fourth chapter of Deuteronomy contains serious warnings identifying with the committing of transgression (sin) by the Israelites and chapter 28 gives a prophetic image of their overall scattering (world-wide dispersion) because of their national sins.

It is into this place of Israel's life that the doctrine of Balaam is presented. Balaam indicated Balak how Israel could be briefly halted from accomplishing God's objective. Balak and his people were encouraged to associate with Israel, and to intermarry with them, in this way making them inadequate for God's service.

This doctrine of Balaam prompted a significant number of the Israelites becoming idolaters and to thinking that as a nation they were secure in God's sovereign plan, they could do however they wanted, or as they pleased without any adverse effect upon them. This was a false security.

Balaamism's Results Today

Let us apply this lesson to ourselves today. There are some professing Christians among us who discuss their security in Christ and announce that it has no effect how they live. Their salvation isn't a limitation on their sinning but turns into a excuse for it. They announce that if one's belief is right, he need not be worried about his conduct.

This has created a conflict among believers because of the extraordinary educating of some with reference to the sovereign grace of God and their absence of conscience toward sin.

With the genuine Christian there are opposite sides to this question similarly as we have found on account of Israel. God's side is given in John 10:28 where we read, "I give unto them eternal life; and they will never perish, neither shall any man pluck them out of my hand." Some people carelessly have stated, "Well, however I can bounce out of His hand."

Such an statement, be that as it may, overlooks the reasonable instructing of the passage. The promise is, "They shall never perish" and the verse in the original reads, "Neither shall any pluck them out of my hand." Neither we ourselves nor anyone else can remove us from the hand of God once we are in it through faith in Christ. Presently, that is God's side. That states our position in Christ. This is something the adversary can't obliterate.

Another reassuring verse is John 6:37 where our Savior promised: "Him that cometh to me I will in no wise cast out." No one can pluck us out, and the Savior won't cast us out. that is one side of this entire subject.

Presently take a look at the opposite side. In depicting His sheep the Savior said in John 10:27 KJV: "My sheep hear my voice, and I know them, and they follow me: And I give unto them eternal life; and they shall never perish." This demonstrates to us that it is His sheep who receive eternal life, the individuals who know Him, hear His voice, and follow Him. They follow Him because they are His. It's anything but an issue of the individuals who should pursue or who may pursue. His sheep are the persons who do follow Him.

A further elaboration on this is given in I John 3:9: "Whosoever is born of God doth not submit sin; for his seed remaineth in him; and he can not sin, because he is born of God."

There are two extremely critical explanations made here. "Whosoever," we are told, "is born of God does not submit sin," or even better "does not practice sin."

At that point it proceeds to state, "for his seed remaineth in him and he can not sin." Christ is the seed in us and He can not sin. The outcome of this is with Christ inhabiting the believer the believer can no longer keep practicing sin in the way be did before he was saved.

We ought remember that even in the apostolic church there were the individuals who made a profession of faith in Christ who as a general rule had no possession of faith in Christ who in all actuality had no possession of Him. Again we read in I John these words: "They went out from us, but they were not of us; fort if they had been of us, they would no doubt have continued with us; but they went out, that they may be made manifest that they were not we all" (I John 2:19 KJV).

We perceive completely that not all who fall into transgression in the church are false professors. The doctrine of Balaam is being practiced in our midst as it was in Israel's initial history and as was seen in apostolic days.

There are individuals who utilize the grace of God as a permit to sin. Israel has been suffering over almost four millenniums for that teaching she held on to as taught by Balaam. In like manner, there are Christians today who have progressed toward becoming companions of the world and therefore have gone under God's disciplinary judgments.

James stated, "Ye adulterers and adulteresses, know ye not that the kinship of the world is ill will with God? Whosoever in this way will be a friendship of the world is enmity with God" (James 4:4). At the point when the genuine Christian advances beside the way of righteousness, he has to answer God for his defiance, his disobedience.

No ifs ands or buts, there are people in our midst today who have been pulled in by the doctrine of the security of the believer but have no genuine faith in their own hearts concerning Christ, and utilize their fancied security as a permit to sin.

Keep in mind that in keeping in touch with the church at Pergamos, the Lord said that they must repent and do their benevolent acts rapidly or He would come and battle against them with the sword of His mouth. God won't tolerate sin in any of His children.

Then again, some of God's very own people may have rejected reality of the believer's security in Christ in light of the free living with respect to some who hold that doctrine. None of us ought to allow ourselves to be robbed of the assurance of salvation in Christ. Let us adhere to the Word of God and live accordingly.

The doctrine as it applies to our places of worship today drives Christians into the transgression of spiritual fornication where they turn out to be neighborly with the world and living for Christ. Experience, we should remember, is an attitude of heart. In spots extraordinary incentive on temporary things and dismisses eternal things.

Some have endeavored to pinpoint experience as wearing specific sorts of dress or driving particular kinds of autos or numerous different things of Galatians 2:20 a similar sort. Worldliness has to do fundamentally with wrong intentions, wrong motives and attitudes. At the point when our motives and attitudes are right, the outward articulation of the life will be right.

The Doctrine Of The Nicolaitanes

The second issue the Lord discovered amiss with the church at Pergamos is communicated in these words: "So hast thou also them that hold the doctrine of the Nicolaitanes, which thing I hate" (Rev. 2:15 ASV). There is little help from the commentaries with respect to what the doctrine of the Nicolaitanes really was. The best response to the issue is found in the Word itself.

The word Nicolaitanes is really two Greek words consolidated, the first being "nikao" signifying "to conquer"; the second is "laos" which means people or "laity." From the prophetic and verifiable historical angel this church speaks to the age which saw the start of the rise of priesthood and the authority of such men over the souls of others.

It is just the same old thing new for men to crave or lust religious power, but it is constantly sad when they do, and the results are constantly insidious. Such disregard the Lord's admonition when He stated, "He that will be the greatest among you, let him be the servant of all."

God says He hates this doctrine of the Nicolaitanes. When the organized church achieved where the clergy were put on a high platform or pedestal and given supreme power over all laity God was grieved and angered. The evil results of this system have been to put in the hands of men the prerogatives that belong only to Christ.

Dr. John Thomas Wylie

He it was who came and provided salvation to us, given on the basis of faith in Him. It isn't dispensed by men at their will but applied to human hearts through faith by the Holy Spirit.

God gave gifted men to the church as per Ephesians 4:11,12 KJV: "And he gave a some, apostles; and a some, prophets; and a some, evangelists; and a some, pastors and teachers." His prupose in this manner is communicated in the following words: "For the perfecting of the saints, for the work of the ministry, for the edifying of the body of Christ."

These men were given to the congregation to develop it, to teach the holy people, to prepare them, and to unite them in the work of the ministry.

In any case, what has occurred during that time is that work of the ministry has come to mean the work of the ministers. A few men known as the "clergy" and frequently called "ministers" are given the responsibility which really has a place with all the Body of Christ. God did not put this issue to a vote and ask his people what their desire was with regard to it.

Here is the thing that He says to the those who have been reconciled to Him and which incudes all who have trusted in Christ: "And all things are of God, who hath reconcileded us to himself by Jesus Christ, and hath given to us the ministry of reconciliation" (II Corinthians 5:18 KJV). This is an task for the whole body of Christ, not for a chosen few.

God does not get rid of human organizations. Such are emdorsed in His Word. What's more, it is likewise true, that there are some whom He has called to invest all their time in His work. One might be an instructor, another an evangelist, and another a preacher and pastor. Yet, the explanation behind such pioneers isn't that they may overwhelm and control other believers, however that they may prepare these believers for work of the ministry.

That is a part of the function of this perusing which God has brought up in nowadays. It isn't just our duty to look to win others for Christ but in also to teach Christians so that they, too, can help spread the good news of our Lord.

A Twofold Sin

The modern sin of Nicolaitanism is twofold from my perspective. There are the individuals who lord over God's hertiage. There are others again who hold their obligation that is theirs as believers to Christ and say that they hire the clergy to do that work for them.

How far this all is from the program of God! You review that our Savior stated, "Ye will get power, after that the Holy Ghost is come upon you: and ye shall be witnesses unto me both in Jerusalem, and in all Judea, and in Samaria, and unto the uttermost part of the earth" (Acts 1:8 KJV). In this He gave His believers both a lical and a world-wide program.

The tendency is, as it generally has been, for individuals to keep the witnessing to a little part or to their very own gathering. So it was with the early church. When we achieve the eighth chapter of Acts we discover the work of God restricted to a great extent to Jerusalem and Judea. A little had infiltrated into Samaria, however the uttermost part of the earth was a long way from hearing the gospel. It had been completely neglected so far.

God allowed persecution to fall upon the Church, and its members "were altogether scattered abroad all through the locales of Judaea and Samaria, aside from the apostles. Along these lines, they that were scattered abroad went everywhere preaching the Word." The "clergy," if we may utilize that term regarding the apostles, remained in Jerusalem while the "laity" spread the gospel out from Judea and Samaria and into different parts.

This is the program that has been pursued on numerous occasions. God has had to allow persecution to come upon His people before they were eager to travel to another country with the message of life.

Afterawhile, in the early church, the clergy not only had authority to run the congregation (church), but soon they became the only interpreters of Scriptures. There came day when they even removed the Bible from the average folks, saying that they couldn't comprehend it. Only the priesthood could decipher the Scriptures. Finally that wound up restricted to a few leaders in the organized church. Such at that point, was the wrongdoing (sin) of the Nicolaitanes, and its evil fruit.

God's warning to Peragamos was, "Repent; or else I will come unto thee quickly, and will fight against them with the sword of my mouth" (Rev. 2:16).

"Repent" intends to turn about, to get some distance from something, and it includes a difference in mentality, a change of attitude, a difference in heart, and a difference as a change of mind.

The "coming of the Lord in this warning isn't the second coming, as we have noted previously; it has to do with disciplinary judgment on those of God's children who defy Him (disobey Him) at a specific time.

For reasons unknown or another, the Word of God isn't going into hearts today with the piercing quality that it should be. There is excessively apathy even among the general population of God. It isn't the desire of the Father to have to discipline in the sense discussed in this verse. He would prefer that we would obey and readily, gladly, fulfill our duties. So we gain from the Scriptures that in the event that we would hear His voice, we ought not solidify (harden) our hearts but rather come to Him.

Pergamos was rebuked for tolerating the teaching of Balaam and the doctrine of the Nicolaitanes. Is it true that we are in anywise blameworthy, guilty of tolerating similar things in our lives and hearts today? At that point we can in no wise hope to get away from His own judgment as expressed here to this church.

Chapter Five

Jesus Christ Speaks To Thyatira

"AND TO THE ANGEL of the church in Thyatira write: These things saith the Son of God, who hath his eyes like a flame of fire, and his feet are like fine brass; I know thy works and charity, and service, and faith, and thy patience, and thy works; and the last to be more than the first.

"Notwithstanding I have a few things against thee, because thou suffered that woman Jezebel, which calleth herself a prophetess, to teach and to seduce my servants to commit fornication, and to eat things sacrificed unto idols. And I gave her space to repent her fornication; and she repented not, Behold, I will cast her into a bed, and them that commit adultery with her into great tribulation, except they repent of their deeds. And I will kill her children with death, and all the churches shall know that I am he which searcheth the reins and hearts: and I will give unto every one of you according to your works."

"But unto you I say, and unto the rest in Thyatira, as many as have not this doctrine, and which have not known the depths of Satan, as they speak; I will put upon you none other burden. But that which ye have already hold fast till I come."

"And he that overcometh, and keepeth my works unto the end, to him I give power over the nations; And he shall rule them with a rod of iron; as the vessels of a potter shall they be broken to shivers; even a I received of my Father. And I will give him the morning star. He that hath an ear, let him hear what the Spirit saith unto the churches" (Rev. 2:18-29 KJV)."

How little most of us of seem to realize Who it is that addresses us in these letters! Men when all is said in done are listening less and less to what God has to say.

At this very time there is controversy among the countries of the earth regarding who speaks with power. The free world seeks America to represent them. This is challenged by Russia who might want to represent all the world. Be that as it may, we all need to tune in to Christ. He is the Alpha and the Omega, the beginning and the end. He began all things and He will bring everything to their consummation. His Word is last, and man ought to figure out how to serve Him with fear and trembling.

In the passage before us Christ is depicted as having eyes like a flame of fire. He has absolute and intimate knowledge of every one of our hearts. He knows the profoundest mysteries or secrets among us.

There is nothing hidden from Him, our flaws, our intentions, our mistakes or whatever else about us.

We can comfort in light of this, for He will give legitimate and proper acknowledgment to all who steadfastly serve Him. Full recognition does not come to us necessarily in this world; and as a rule none at all is given in this world to a significant number of God's servants. However, God knows these things, and records all of our heart's devotion and service to Him. One day He will reward us for our faithfulness.

His feet, we are told, resemble fine brass; this speaks to us of coming judgment. For a few conditions there is no cure spare judgment. Apostasy, for instance, which is an intentional, deliberate denying of and falling far from truth, closes just in judgment.

Those alluded to in Romans chapter one who "hold down truth in unrighteousness" will be judged. In Hebrews we discover that "if we sin willfully after that we have received the knowledge of truth, there remaineth no more sacrifice for sins, But a specific frightful looking for of judgment and red hot outrage, which will eat up the enemies" (Heb. 10:26,27 KJV).

In the Book of the Revelation Christ is revealed, uncovered as the One who brings judgment. However how delicately men treat this issue. There is "no fear of God before their eyes." And this irreverance toward God even characterizes many Christians.

We dare not ignore the spiritual law communicated in the 6th chapter of Galatians where we learn that God isn't mocked, that "at whatsoever a man soweth, that will he likewise reap." If men sow to the flesh, they will reap of the flesh; if they sow to the Spirit, they will reap of the Spirit. The last assessment of whether we have served in the flesh or in the Spirit lies with God, and we will be rewarded or lose rewards accordingly.

God knows our works as this passage in the Book of Revelation appears. Nothing is

Dr. John Thomas Wylie

ignored. This is given us by method for support to safeguard in accommodation and quietude in administration for Him. God is honorable and won't neglect the positive qualities in the things that we do. He will laud us for even the little things we have done right.

In the event that men, then again, see a couple of things being fouled up by somebody, they are slanted to denounce the man's entire life. This is a dismal situation. We see a man whom God might utilize, and he commits an error maybe just of judgment, however immediately a significant number of his kindred believers censure and disavow him. Since he fails in one period of his life, they assume that nothing he does means God.

Paul needed to confront this trouble with the Corinthian believers. He recognized himself to be a negligible man and at risk to blunder and sin, and rested his straightforwardness in God's hand. He realized that one day God will bring to light all the mystery things of men's souls and show outward activities in their actual light.

In making a decision about Sodom, God did not disregard the way that Lot and individuals from his family unit should have been saved from the destruction going to fall upon the urban areas of the fields. Also, however there were a huge number of individuals, perhaps millions, who were profane, indecent, and unholy before the surge, God did not overlook the one man and his family who, regardless of their condition, satisfied God with their lives.

Judas, who denied and double-crossed, betrayed the Lord Jesus Christ, was offered space to repent. He even brought back the selling out cash and cast it at the feet of the priests. I am certain as far as I could tell that the Lord would have overlooked Judas if he had accompanied a repentant heart. He was loaded up with regret for his shrewd deed, but evidently he didn't look for the pardoning God would gladly have provided.

Thyatira's Love

Thyatira had, something like, a proportion of love for the Lord. The word interpreted "charity" ought to be love. Thyatira had what Ephesus had cleared out. Here was a church that was serving Christ out of an love for Him, conceivably having paid attention to the warning given to the Ephesian church.

Faithfulness also portrayed this gathering. They were diligent in service and did not hestitate to give some cold water in the Savior's name. A few people are prepared to spread an expansive meal feast (banquet) however ease back to do the littler things that truly demonstrate their love for Christ. It is once in a while less demanding to preach to a group than it is to minister to an individual soul.

The emphasis today among us is on the huge groups and the showy projects. Be that as it may, God sees the easily overlooked details and gives tribute in like manner. The church at Thyatira had been working for the Lord quite a while. They had not left their first love; but rather, that love was developing and expanding as the days passed by.

So should it be with us in our service. We ought not be happy with what we did to improved the situation for the Lord yesterday, but seek today to be dedicated and, if conceivable, complete a far better activity. We should work and walk and live with the Lord and develop in the knowledge of Him constantly and reliably.

In any case, the church at Thyatira was not faultless. It had settled down in the world, and in settling down in the world, it settled down in transgression (sin). The spiritual state of Thyatira helps us to remember the parable our Savior spoke concerning the woman who place leaven in the dinner. This was sin in this church. The present state of mind of the world and the climate in church circles today is for us all to be tolerant toward wrongdoing (sin).

Be that as it may, this must never be permitted, we enable a little leaven to enter in, it will leaven the whole lump. We who are God's people must be always on the caution against the coming in of evil.

Soon it will penetrate the whole, causing disunity and making our service ineffective.

The Woman Jezebel

The believers in Thyatria also allowed a prophetess by the name of Jezebel to prosper in their midst and to instruct and lead God's people astray. This detestable woman presented idolatry which God called "fornication," obviously spiritual fornication, thus He stated, "I will cast her in a bed, and them that commit adultery with her into an incredible tribulation, except from they repent of their deeds.

I will slaughter her children with death; and every one of the churches shall know that I am he which searcheth the reins and hearts: and I will give unto all of you according to your works." These are strong words, yet they were spoken to a organized church. There were unbelievers in the midst, certainly, Jezebel was one; yet the Christians permitted her, without challenge on their part, to show her devilish, wicked doctrines.

We see a comparable state of mind in numerous churches today. We are advised to be increasingly "tolerant" towards individuals who don't see eye to eye with us. Obviously "love" to such people implies tolerance of sin. The facts confirm that God has never embraced nor pushed abuse of the individuals who don't hold to the true faith. The individuals who take up the sword, our Lord lets us know, will die by the sword.

Then again He has made it clear that Christians are not to permit false teachers into the fellowship of the churches. Also, bargaining with the world won't win the world. The general population on the planet are so frustrated with the bargains they see among their very own group that they have no regard for a Christian who might trade off his imperative message with an end goal to win those contradicted to him.

In any case, it is a typical thing to see enrollment drives in churches outfitted to duplicate individuals yet not individuals who are born again. The New Testament instructs that the individuals who are saved should connect themselves with Bible-believing churches. In that way believers can join in service and worship together; however we conflict with the bearings of the Lord when we bring unbelievers into our midst and hope in this way that we can reach them for Christ. Invariably they will do as Jezebel did and corrupt our fellowships.

The principles in the Word of God are. We read, "Be ye not unequally yoked together with unbelievers...Wherefore turn out from among them, and be ye seperate, saith the Lord, and touch not the unclean thing; and I will receive you" (II Cor. 6:14-17 KJV).

The Historic Jezebel

For a far reaching image of Jezebel's character and direct and her vicious end read from I Kings 16:28 all the way to the end of the book and after that the later part of the ninth part of II Kings. Jezebel, we find, was an idolator, an adherent of the false god Baal. She made a twofold assault upon the profound pioneers of the true God in Israel.

She as a matter of first importance attempted to motivate them to trade off their testimony. At that point, those she couldn't convince to bargain their faith, she oppressed until the very end.

Presently, in Ahab's family unit was one named Obadiah who had the obligation of dealing with Ahab's private concern issues. Obadiah was a man who "feared the Lord extraordinarily," and when Jezebel was looking to murder God's prophets, Obadiah saved a hundred of them with bread and water" ((Kings 18:4). From this we discover that Jezebel was not by any stretch of the imagination effective in stepping out the love of the true God.

In any case, all through Israel as of now, idolatry prospered, and all as a result of the malevolent blend of religions presented by Jezebel.

It isn't difficult to see a comparative condition in our churches today. Such a large number of church groups feel that they should make their program alluring to the world by trading off with common principles. The extraordinary accentuation on the planet is amusement (entertainment); thusly, numerous holy places have attempted to put on a program that will entertain instead of convict of sin and lead individuals to Christ and build up them in the faith.

The world is far superior ready to give the sort of entertainment common individuals need. The church, when it tries to rival the world on this plane, is totally strange and unfit to deliver. It is right for Christians to have a specific measure of diversion relying upon what is implied by entertainment. If it is only a question of killing time, as individuals say, the Christian has no opportunity to kill.

Everytime we kill time we are killing souls. We are not finding a way to capture their descending adventure. It is pitiful to feel that indeed the program Jezebel initiated such a significant number of years prior is discovering achievement amidst God's people today.

She also ruined government and utilized it to maintain her false instructing. In any case, it is the piece of idyllic equity that it was at long last government that disposed of her as a result of the debasements she brought into the life of

Dr. John Thomas Wylie

Israel. She was offered "space to repent of her fornication; and she repented not."

An exceptionally startling certainty is that numerous bogus religions of the present day were started by women. This is no arraignment of women, for without authentic women of God the work would be enormously obstructed. In numerous mission fields there are five women evangelists for each man minister. Also, in our very own nation there are a bigger number of women who go to church than men.

In the meantime a considerable lot of the bogus religions of the present day have been started by women who have gone off into "special revelations."

We should be watchful of the individuals who come to us with exceptional helps, unique keys, new revelations, and new shrouded methods of insight which are not the spiritual things of God but rather the profound things of Satan. The church and Christians today need to return to what the Bible teaches.

One of the best adversaries of the gospel, in any case, is higher criticism, which was begun by men, not a woman. Higher feedback has rejected the supernatural occurrences of the Word, continually having some conceivable clarification for them that interests to unbelieving hearts.

I remember an assemblage in Clarksville, Tennessee close where I was raised for a part of my life. There came an evangelist who was captured in Modernism. He needed to go along his "new learning" to the congregation not realizing that the specific gathering he was addressing had numerous Bible scholars in it.

One day in looking to clarify away the supernatural occurrence of the sustaining of the five thousand, he expressed that Christ was such a dynamic instructor and identity that the general population sat and tuned in to him for a considerable length of time without understanding the progression of time and the way that they were ravenous. He so sustained them with scholarly and profound sustenance that they didn't require any physical nourishment.

At the point when this evangelist was through giving this clarification a young girl, six, maybe seven years old, stood up and stated, "Preacher, I'd like to ask you a question. If that is the manner in which Jesus nourished those individuals, where did He get the twelve bushels full that were left finished?" It took a young girl to demonstrate the silliness of the educating of the higher critics.

In any case, this is normal today, this matter of looking to clarify the Bible on an absolutely human dimension. Men disregard the way that spiritual things are profoundly recognized. Scriptural things are Scripturally, and spiritually discerned. It is only as the Spirit of God brightens our hearts that we can comprehend the things of God.

Men ordinarily can't comprehend the infinite and the eternal. Who could clarify that God never had a beginning and never will have an end? We have a beginning, but we will never have an end. We will either spend time everlasting in damnation (hell) or in paradise. That relies on the preparation and decision we make concerning Christ here upon this world.

We should examine ourselves to check whether we are giving our cash and our opportunity to associations and endeavors that are compromising the truth of God, rather than proclaiming completely the whole counsel of God. We will find that this blend of Christianity and the world with its human methods of insight isn't satisfying to God. We should turn back to Christ and His truth.

Whose Yoke Do We Wear?

In II Corinthians 6 KJV, "yoke" is now and then misconstrued. The Lord does not plan us to end up loners and pull back ourselves from other individuals despite the fact that we are to be discrete in our association from the world and from unbelievers. Rather, we are to take Christ's burden upon us and return into the fields to come to the unsaved with the gospel.

A burden connotes the authoritative of ourselves with somebody or something. If that it is the wrong individual or the wrong program, we are unequally burdened (yoke). For a Christian man to look for an unbeliever as his significant other or a Christian woman to look for an unbeliever as her better half, is to be unequally burdened (unequally yoked).

For a Christian to look for an accomplice in business who is an unbeliever, will spell trouble for them both. The equivalent is valid with respect to church connections. In the event that a Bible-believing Christian joins himself to an unbelieving church that would make an unequal burden.

In any of these cases the Christian would put himself under commitment to get things done

Dr. John Thomas Wylie

against his very own still, small voice and faith; and, which would be similarly terrible, he would not have the capacity to do things that he knows he should do.

Over against the unequal yoke we are welcome to take Christ's yoke upon us. It is a simple yoke, as He said. In this yoke with Christ, we don't do the things the flesh wants but the things the Holy Spirit wants. We are yoked together with Christ and He as our Head guides us and instructs us and where to go.

Similarly as my hand is a part of my body and can't act autonomously of whatever remains of the body, especially of the head, just so is the Christian yoked to Christ under the direction of Christ.

In the unequal yoke, one will pull one way and one the other. This will result in compromise or in dissatisfaction, frustration or both; however at last it would imply that God would be the true loser. Righteousness has no fellowship with unrighteousness. Light has no place of compromise with darkness.

It is no big surprise, that we read: "Come out from among them, and be ye separate, saith the Lord, and touch not the unclean thing; and I will receive you, And will be a Father unto you, and ye shall be my sons and daughters, saith the Lord Almighty. Having therefore these promises dearly beloved, let us cleanse ourselves from all filthiness of the flesh and spirit, protecting holiness in the fear of God" (II Cor. 6:17, 18-7:1 ASV).

We are in the world but we are not to be of the world. When our Savior was here upon the earth He ate with sinners. He even ate with a portion of the Pharisees who were the Modernists of that day. There are numerous Christian circles today where our Lord would be scrutinized for doing what He did; however we should remember that in none of these activities did He yoke Himself or compromise His message with unbelievers.

We can see a similar truth on account of Elijah. He called upon Ahab to bring the general population of Israel together to Mount Carmel to discover exactly who the genuine God truly was. Elijah was yoked to God, not to Ahab, in this challenge. Ahab was a necessary means to the end, for it was through him that a group was assembled.

Elijah was in charge of the spiritual exercise. Keep in mind that in these issues God contemplates the thought processes of the heart, and some of the time what may appear as though a compromise

Dr. John Thomas Wylie

yoke with respect to some servant of God might be no yoke at all except basically a genuine method of reaching certain ones for Jesus Christ.

Judgment On Jezebel

A severe judgment was announced against Jezebel. The Lord stated, "See, I will cast into a bed, and them that commit infidelity with her into incredible tribulation, except they repent of their deeds." When individuals are snoozing on a bed they are unaware of things around them. They are loose and unconcerned about the course of occasions.

In light of this setting such false teachers and leaders will be in a sort of spiritual languor (spiritual sluggishness) and won't just hoodwink (deceive) others however will be cheated (deceived) themselves. The record is that "evil men and seducers will wax worse and more worse, deceiving and being deceived" (II Tim. 3:13 KJV).

The individuals who submit infidelity (adultery) with Jezebel are to be thrown into incredible tribulation except from they repent. These, without uncertainty, are the unregenerate. Over against this is the promise in the third chapter of Revelation to adherents: "Because thou hast kept the word of my patience, I likewise will keep thee from the hour of temptation (great tribulation), which will come upon all the world, to try them that dwell upon the earth" (v. 10).

This should help settle one of the contentions that are so overflowing among Bible believers of the present time. These two Scriptures reveal to us evidently who will go into the tribulation and who won't. The unregenerate, the individuals who are not born again, will be thrown into tribulation. The individuals who are born again, as indicated by our Savior's own promise, will not pass through the great tribulation.

So severe will be this judgment that the unregenerate individuals from the organized churches will have no inquiry regarding what is transpiring. God who looks through the reins and the hearts knows the genuine spiritual status of each person, and each will receive as per his or her works. This does not mean salvation by works, but rather believers will be rewarded by their works, and unbelievers will suffer degrees of punishment according to their works.

In any case, there was a remainder in Thyatira who did not have the doctrine of Jezebel and who did not know the profundities of Satan. No other burden was to be set upon them. They are appealed to, be that as it may, to hold fast until Jesus Christ comes.

This is a message for us today, for Thyatira's conditions are being re-established afresh in our midst. These are times of dormancy and of chilliness and of compromise. A large number of God's people are missing out with Him, however, but let us determine to hold fast that which we have. God wants to be able to give us the crown He has promised us. We must tune in to what He says. God hates neutrality. He wants us to take sides-His side- and be all-in-all for Him.

Spiritual Retrogression

In various places in the Scriptures God gives us a record of spiritual declension with respect to men or gatherings. On account of Achan, the record of whose wrongdoing is given in Joshua 7, we discover that he initially took a look at the spoils, coveted them, took them, and lastly hid them in the earth. Sin works in that way.

First there is the intrigue through the eye entryway, at that point covetousness emerges in the heart to where we take what we need. At long last, conscience smites us, and we endeavor to conceal the insidious thing we have done.

In first Psalm we see a progression in wrongdoing (sin) too. We find there that the blessed man is the person who walks not in the direction of the profane, nor obstructs the heathen (sinner), and does not sit in the counsel of the sinner. By disclosing to us what the faithful man does not do, we realize what the wicked man does do; and in this dynamic decrease we discover him first walking, then standing, lastly sitting among the unbelievers.

The ungodly man most importantly talks about the wrong things, for he walks in the insight of the profane. At that point he starts to obstruct sinners, lastly he is given a changeless (permanent) seat in the place of sin. This isn't just a warning to unbelievers shows what can occur in the life of a Christian who gives way to wrong desires and wrong company.

Retrogression In The Churches

In these letters to the seven churches, we locate that five of them were edited for evil conduct. Two of them were definitely not.

Dr. John Thomas Wylie

On account of the first, we found that it cleared out (left) its first love. They didn't lose it however purposely abandoned it. The service, which was abundant, was done as an issue of obligation as opposed to emerging out of adoration. The motive was wrong.

Love is a constraining power which is fundamental in the cause for the Lord and is also vital really form shape of a home. It takes love with respect to the spouse to cook for quite a while to deal with her family and her significant other and stay aware of the ordinary tasks of homemaking. Where such love is available, home life is charming; and what under different conditions may be drudgery moves toward becoming delight on account of the affection back of it. Devoted children who discover dutifulness a joy are the individuals who have love persuading them.

At the point when married life, be that as it may, turns into an obligation since affection is gone, soon the home is in threat.

Thus it is so in the work of the Lord. If our service springs from our every day fellowship with Him through the Word and through supplication then our service will be a delight and a pleasure.

To the church of Pergamos our Lord spoke against free living (loose living). At the point when the principal love is gone, and those dependable are obstinate in their rebellion, soon unadulterated benchmarks vanish and insidious practices assume control.

The equivalent can be found in a home. Where it is only obligation that calls soon detachment of living can show itself in either the spouse or the wife. They get their eyes on another person. Where the rationale isn't right in the Christian life, self sneaks in and Christ is closed out. At that point we look for self-respect, and power for self, and self-magnificence, and the entire life bases on what we need and what we appreciate.

With love for Christ gone, it is nothing unexpected that principles, for example, the tenet of Baalam and of the Nicolaitanes sneaks in. In the fourth church, Thyatira, we discover the spirit of compromise which prompts "spiritual fornication" winds up noticeable. When we come to Sardis we find the spiritual life is deteriorated to the point that Christianity is just a name with the nurturing rule gone. We read, "thou hast a name that thou livest, but are dead."

Dr. John Thomas Wylie

Religious form and love of Christ as a decent man, are substituted for the living Son of God, however the mystery of the gospel which Paul was given to preach to the world is totally overlooked, or forgotten.

The end is achieved when we read of the church of Laodicea, "I know thy works, that thou works, that are neither cool nor hot: I would thou wert cold or hot. So then since thou are lukewarm, and neither chilly nor hot, I will spew thee out of my mouth." That which began with the leaving of the first love closes in dynamic active apostasy.

The church that started to preach the message of life turns into the church that is against the Christ of the Bible. It's not an anti-religious movement but an anti-Christian movement. It contradicts the things of God and leaves Christ outside knocking asking permission or consent to enter.

With regards to these dynamic phases of sin, leading to apostasy, we have God's statement of progressive judgment. To the first church the warning was given that God would come and remove the "candle out of his place, aside from thou repent."

This talks about the removal of the work of the Holy Spirit from their midst. Then follows judgment by the Word in which the Lord pronounces that He would come and battle against them with the sword of His mouth. The third judgment is that sinners would be thrown into a bed with the false prophetess and furthermore into great tribulation.

By and by, in the majority of this, God gives such people chance to repent.

Then in the third chapter we are faced with this warning: "I will come unto thee as a thief." This is sure judgment with no further warning to be given. At long last will come absolute eternal separation from God. Rejection of Him when persisted in will prompt the second death.

It may be that Christ is outside your heart's entryway today thumping, knocking, requesting to come in. Will you not say "Yes" to Him today? What you require is Christ, not religion. Give Him Access, Let Him In!

Chapter Six

Jesus Christ Speaks To Sardis

"And unto the angel of the church in Sardis write; These things saith he that hath the seven Spirits of God, and the seven stars; I know thy works, that thou hast a name that thou livest, and art dead. Be watchful, and strengthen the things which remain, that are ready to die: for I have not found thy works perfect before God."

"Remember therefore now thou hast received and heard, and hold fast, and repent. If therefore thou shalt not watch, I will come on thee as a thief, and thou shalt not know what hour I will come upon thee."

"Thou hast a few names even in Sardis which have not defiled garments; and they shall walk with me in white: for they are worthy. He that overcometh, the same shall be clothed in white raiment; and I will not blot out his name out of the book of life, but I will confess his name before my Father, and before his angels. He that hath an ear, let him hear what the Spirit saith unto the churches" (Rev. 3:1-6).

Here was a church with a decent reputation among men. They had a name that they lived, yet in God's sight they were dead. It helps us to remember our very own day here in the United States to have a place with a church is exceptionally important. Church enrollment stands (in a few churches) at an unsurpassed high, however what is the personal satisfaction proof among us?

God in evaluating the church at Sardis stated, "Thou art dead." They indicated much action as if they were alive, however they were quite dead. Their activities had individuals trusting that the Sardis church was alive; God, in any case, did not discover its works impeccable before Him.

They had not displayed their bodies as living sacrifices to God and in this way communicated in their lives what was holy and acceptable to Him (Rom. 12:1,2 KJV). At the end of the day, they were not meeting God's prerequisites. They had set up their very own standards and discarded of God's.

Dr. John Thomas Wylie

Searching Questions

Let us be truthful and straightforward with ourselves. Is this an picture of the church we have a place with or we belong to? Or then again an picture of own hearts? When we come to break bread at the Lord's Supper (Communion), do we really value the spiritual substance of that dinner? Or on the other hand is it simply an enthusiastic involvement in which we feel that in the event that we are sufficiently sincere enough we are pleasing God?

Is our church form of worship true worship? Do we truly honor Jesus Christ in it? Is our Bible perusing driving us to a more profound learning, a deeper knowledge of Him and to be more obedient to His Word? We feed on the flesh and blood of the Son of God, as the figure is used in John chapter 6, when we read and meditate on the Word and commune with God through it.

Somebody has said that we can tell how popular a church is by what number of individuals attend on a Sunday morning. The prevalence of the minister is demonstrated by the individuals who go to the church on Sunday evening, Sunday night and different occasions other than morning worship.

Are our gifts for the Lord's service gifts of obligation or gifts of adoration? Is it true that they are the declaration of our own hearts adoration? Do we give a portion of our salary with the expectation that God will love us for it? God loves a cheerful giver (II Cor.9:7 KJV). A gift to God exhibited based on the basis of duty may not be registered in paradise.

Do we so love the Lord that we buckle down (work hard) for Him and sacrifice so as to give more for His work? Keep in mind, genuine service is service that originates from the heart. The congregation at Sardis, most likely, had expressed occasions for supplication. In any case, did these supplications reach paradise? Or then again would they say they were only an assembling of fine words and smooth sounding sentences? Supplication is substantially more than asking God for something.

Prayer at best is a fellowship, a meditating about the things of God, speaking to Him and permitting and allowing Him to speak to us, and afterwards, letting our requests flow from the burdens He lays upon our hearts.

We have to think about our music and what it truly amounts to. A church might be exceptionally specific about the interpretation of the melodies. It might have a very much prepared (well-trained) choir ready to sing a portion of the more complicated religious and Christian music, however does that choir exalt Jesus Christ?

It is conceivable to talk about being honored with music that has nothing to do with the Word of God at all. It might soothe us; it many stir us; it might make us feel at peace within; but that isn't what music taking care of business is for. It is so natural to appreciate singing and to appreciate certain melodies while never going into the genuine importance of the message.

It is anything but difficult to sing "Rescue the perishing, care for the dying" in a missionary service when our hearts have been touched, however, do we truly respond to these things? Do we have a name that we live and are dead?

n our church business meetings fine-sounding goals are passed, and the advancement of the congregation looks great on paper. There are such huge numbers of new individuals thus much has been given for this work and that work. Be that as it may, what amount of genuine fruitage is there for God? Numbers don't generally recount the story.

What amount more like Jesus Christ are the individuals from your gathering now than they were a year back? Is there sympathy for souls among them? We need to state with Paul, "That I might know him (Jesus Christ) and the power of his resurrection," but what number of us need to participate with Him when He speaks about the fellowship of Christ's sufferings?

We have to look past the immediate earthly contacts and environment and understand that we have responsibilities before God. What sort reputation do we have in paradise? Will the Head of the Church, the Lord Jesus Christ, compliment us for the work we are doing? Is our calling certifiable? Keep in mind that God said to the congregation at Sardis: "I know thy works, that thou hast a name that thou livest, and art dead." God forbid that that ought to be said of any of us.

It is really possible to be alive and dead at the same time? The church at Sardis was. A graphic picture of their condition is given in Matthew: "When the unclean spirit is gone out of a man, he walketh through dry places, seeking rest, and findeth none. Then he saith, I will return into my house from whence I came out; and when he is come, he findeth it empty, swept, and garnished.

Then goeth he and taketh with himself seven other spirits more wicked than himself, and they enter in and dwell there: and the last state of that man is worse than the first. Even so shall it be also unto this wicked generation" (Matt. 12:43-45).

This description fits a lot of supposed Christendom today. An extraordinary arrangement that bears the outward similarity to Christianity is something decorated by human reconstruction but void of Divine Life.

Strengthen What Remains

Sardis was warned to fortify (strengthen) the things that remained. We also may very much notice what was said to that church. God let them know, and He is telling us, to hear His Word, and to be completely wakeful and alarm to what He says. We are the offspring of the day, not of the night; subsequently, we ought to be up and going for the Lord.

in the event that there is whatever is more clear than another as to Satan's present assault on the Church, it is his accomplishment in quieting an extraordinary piece of it to lay down concerning the second coming of Christ. However things around us are going on so quick, world occasions of such dynamite greatness occurring before our own one of a kind eyes, that Jesus could come and remove His Church at any minute.

When the call of the Bridegroom came by Matthew 25, just five of the ten virgins were prepared. The facts confirm that all rested for a period, but when the cry was heard, they all stirred however just five were set up to enter in with the Bridegroom. The other five had a calling as it were.

God isn't deceived nor inspired by any outward demonstrate any of us may make. He knows the heart and realizes that a large number of alleged Christian exercises today are vacant and pointless. At the point when the general population of Sardis were warned to fortify the things that remained, God expected them to comprehend that they were to enable Him to return life again into the vacant structures they were utilizing.

If that they supplicated, they were to implore in the Spirit. On the off chance that they sang, they were to sing in the Spirit. In the event that they worshiped, they were to worship in the Spirit, and not make it a period of joke.

So it is with us. Give us a chance to see that our congregation exercises and our demeanor of worship are veritable. Let our singing and our giving all spring from the thought process of love for Christ.

For the individuals who serving through melody, it isn't sufficient for them to have great voices, to verbalize well, and to try to translate legitimately the message in the tune, however these things are great and attractive in themselves. The focal point ought to be to glorify Christ.

In our church organizations we are not to disregard our committees and study gatherings, and the creation of plans and projects. There is nothing amiss with these things in themselves. They are not taboo, but rather they should all be carried on in the strength and knowledge of the Holy Spirit.

There are three such short Scripture verses which I have found to give a safe guide for every single earthly inquiry. The first is I Corinthians 10:31 RSV: "Do all to the glory of God." Then in Ephesians 5:20 ASV we read, "Give thanks in all things." Finally, in Colossians 3:17 the admonition is: "Do all in his name." Let us then give glory to God in all things, express gratefulness in all things and do everything in His name.

God perceives the outward symbols of service and the conduct of issues of our organized Christian gatherings. In any case, He doesn't need us to be happy with insignificant facades. In the event that the outer communicates the spiritual strength and glory of the internal quality of life, it is good. In the event that the lesson contains a living message that makes it a message, God will utilize it. If that the tune passes on a message, sing it.

A Warning

It is in accordance with this believed the notice is given: "If therefore thou shalt not watch, I will come on thee as a thief, and thou shalt not know what hour I will come upon thee." This isn't the second happening to Christ. This is happening upon men all of a sudden and in mystery to remove something that is profitable. A criminal comes in the night to remove important things.

A similar sort of warning was allowed in the second chapter as we have noted: "Remember therefore from whence thou art fallen, and repent,

Dr. John Thomas Wylie

and do the first works; or else I will come unto thee quickly, and will remove thy candle out of his place, except thou repent."

This us a genuine business with God, and we should consider it important. Except if we submit to God and give Him the glory, He will remove the power from our midst.

Also, the visitation alludes to the removal of that which is valuable. To have the power of God given to us and afterward to fail Him is to sin against Him. He won't be mocked, and the individuals who reliably come fail Him will lose their power. There is excessively playing church; God requests reality.

Where is the power of protest in the congregation today? We once had it in our land. Sunday was a day we gave over totally service and to worship. There were in every case a few people in the community, obviously, who might not adjust; but rather now the world has filled Sunday with its entertainments, and the church is left far behind.

Keep in mind, the thief comes when we least expecting him. He comes at a time we are insensible of (ignorant of), and we don't understand that something valuable is gone until the point that it is past the point of no return.

One exceptionally regular risk we should stay away from is that of applying these facts to some congregation other than our own, or some heart other than our own. We should question as to whether there isn't something here for us, that we may take in more accurately to walk with our Lord. We can see side effects in a few places of worship noted for their conventionality of their floating into dead universality.

The spiritually deadness is set apart by their criticisms of others, and their blame finding with respect to individual believers. To push accuracy of principle is great, but that there is no life to correspond with the doctrine, we have what is appropriately called dead orthodoxy.

Neither must we measure spirituality as far as substantial quantities of people going to gatherings, great finances, and organizations, for the sentence of death might be composed over the whole.

God's Remnant

There is another message here that we should not neglect. All down through the ages, from the time of Adam's transgression (sin) on, God has never abandoned Himself without a remnant. Some place on the earth, regardless of how dark the age, and this is very much shown in history from what we call the Dark Ages, God has had a people who honored Him.

To Sardis the Lord stated, "Thou hast a few names even in Sardis which have not defiled their garments; and they will walk with me in white: for they are worthy. He that overcometh, the same will be clothed in white raiment; and I will not blot out his name out of the book of life, but I will confess his name before my Father, and before his angels. He that hath an ear, let him hear what the Spirit saith unto the churches."

It may not be for us to state who these are in present day Christian circles, yet we realize that God knows who His people are. He realizes who are the faithful ones, the individuals who have not soiled their garments. They may not be perceived by the world being to a congregation that is alive and serving God, but in His sight they are. What's more, all things considered, it is His commendation that matters.

An uncommon reward is offered to the faithful remnant. "They will walk with me in white" in God's promise. We turn to the nineteenth chapter of Revelation, and read in verse 7; "Let us be glad and rejoice, and give honour to him: for the marriage of the Lamb is come, and his wife hath made herself ready." Just what is implied here is clarified in the following words: "And to her was granted that she should be arrayed in fine linen, clean and white: for the fine linen is the righteousness (actually righteousness, or righteous acts) of holy people."

There is an uncommon garment of righteousness we get through having had faith in Him, but this wedding piece of clothing will be one which His Bride has shaped through her very own righteous acts.

Four Tests

There are four tests that we can make to demonstrate regardless of whether or not there is life in a church or in an individual Christian. First there will be development (growth). That does not really mean a development (growth) in membership, for that can emerge out of the congregation's being well known without its being alive. It is somewhat a spiritual growth or development on part of the individual Christians and the church.

Obviously, we will search for individuals to be born again as the result of the testimony of believers, but that won't be the primary thought in the matter of development (growth).

It may make us do some heart seeking without anyone else in the event that we were to not especially the solicitations that are made in some of our prayer gatherings. Some of them, in truth a large number of them, are of an individual sort, basing on the individual needs of those in the gathering. Now and again I have discovered every one of the solicitations were for the physical soundness of people and not a single prayer for a wayward soul. My heart has lamented as I have thought and thought about whether that was the manner in which I prayed as well.

Secondly, there will be compassion. A living church is loaded up with the love for God on the grounds that every believer has had the love for God shed abroad in his heart by the Holy

Spirit (Rom. 5:5 KJV). This love will drive us to individual soul winning. Or on the other hand should God order us among the dead? Is it accurate to say that we are looking to our pastor to do everything? At the point when love is lacking, with regards to, the adoration for souls will be lacking.

Where there is love there will likewise be the unity of the Spirit, as we read in the fourth chapter of Ephesians. The Spirit unites the general population of God as one under Christ. Where there is difficulty, and quarreling, and slandering, there is loss of spiritual power, death rather than spiritual life.

In the fourth place, there will be healthy feelings as to life and love. There will weeping with the individuals who weep, and cheering with the individuals who celebrate. Such healthy and certifiable feeling is preposterous in an air of death. The Christian's euphoria will convey what needs be in melody from one perspective, and on the other with tears for the wayward and lost. There will be distress for disappointment, and grieving over disregard of the Lord Jesus Christ.

There can be, obviously, unwholesome feelings, wild energies of various types produced from the false conviction that these are confirmations of Christian euphoria and the Spirit's presence. These won't be found, nonetheless, where genuine spiritual power is.

We should return to the Word spiritual nourishment. We can no more grow in the Christian life than in the physical in the event that we deny ourselves the correct spiritual nourishment. God's Word is our nourishment, so given us a chance to eat it that we may grow in this way.

Chapter Seven

Jesus Christ Speaks To Philadelphia

THE CHURCH IN PHILADELPHIA is one of the two with which the Lord finds no specific blame. This does not imply that any of us should feel that there is no requirement for watchful assessment of our activities or intentions. The past letters we have considered would show that we should be always on the alert.

The message to Philadelphia reads: "And to the angel of the church in Philadelphia write; These things saith he that is holy, he that is true, he that hath the key of David, he that openeth, and no man shutteth; and shutteth, and no man openeth; I know thy works: behold, I have set before thee an open door, and no man can shut it: for thou hast a little strength, and hast kept my word, and hast not denied my name. Behold, I will make them of the synagogue of Satan, which say they are Jews, and are not, but do lie; behold, I will make them to come and worship before thy feet, and to know that I have loved thee.

Because thou has kept the word of my patience, I also will keep thee from the hour of temptation, which shall come upon all the world, to try them that dwell upon the earth.

Behold, I come quickly: hold that fast which thou hast, that no man take thy crown. Him that overcometh will I make a pillar in the temple of my God, and he shall go no more out; and I will write upon him the name of my God and the name of the city of my God, which is new Jerusalem, which cometh down out of heaven from my God: and I will write upon him my new name. He that hath an ear, let him hear what the Spirit saith unto the churches" (Rev. 3:7-13 KJV).

Character Of The Writer

It is constantly necessary that we examine ourselves by the One who writes to these churches. He is the Holy One and True. Such is His character. His official position is shown in that He is of the ancestry (lineage) of David, has the key of David, and will sit upon David's throne in the last days. Jesus Christ also has authoritative power, for He opens and no man closes; He closes and no man can open.

Dr. John Thomas Wylie

This character has two sides to it. First, He is holy, speaking about that which is inside (within). This advises us that our thought processes should be checked as to their validity. We have to learn in the event that they are a consequence of the new birth, and of the indwelling Christ. He is holy, and the individuals who are individuals from His family will bear His resemblance.

He is also true, and this has to do with His outward actions. His outward actions conform with His internal character. What He does and says are predictable with what He is.

Does our outward life conform to the image of Christ inside us? Or on the other hand do we put on a show of holiness which isn't sacredness in any way? What we are can speak so loud that the world can't hear what we say. For us to be powerful witnesses, we should have Christ indwelling us, as well as our conduct should express His righteousness.

The present laxity among Christians is because of a breakdown in character. We don't feed upon Christ as the Scriptures show; thus, we miss out in our testimony. But, when there is authentic faithfulness to Him and genuine fellowship with

Him, at that point our outward actions will pull in individuals to Him.

An evangelist companion once said to me, "To be, could really compare to do, for the doing originates from the being." We can't be what we should separated from the Word of God. Except if we set aside opportunity to think about it and absorb it consistently. Our lives will need power and righteousness.

Christ isn't just flawless or perfect in character, He is likewise perfect in power, perfect in authority. He has the right to the throne of David by virtue of the virgin birth which place Him in the heredity as well as the lineage of David. Moreover, through spiritual conquest on the cross He has rule over all realms, forces, principalities, and powers.

His throne will combine heavenly authority with earthly authority. When our Lord rules on this earth He will be God show in the flesh, making His residence among men and controlling and reigning in righteousness. Presently He addresses men through His Word and through His Spirit and through the Church; But later on (in the future kingdom) He will speak to the world in Person.

At that point see additionally His power of administration. When He opens the entryway no man can close it. When He close an entryway no man can open it. There is no veto over His authority. He not just has the right to act; He has the ability to act.

We would be a lot more grounded Christians today if a portion of these certainties ended up implanted in our souls. Our Savior isn't only able to do, But He is dynamic in fulfilling His plans and purposes.

Responsibility Of The Open Door

Our responsibility, when He opens a door for us is to go through it. He can in any case open or close doors paying little heed to the movement of governments and the resistance of men, evil presence propelled however some of them without a doubt are.

I recall when Russia, for instance, had the iron curtain. However God utilized the radio and different intends to get in behind that curtain.

In different lands, which for some reason has in the past made it troublesome for the Christian missionary to enter, God still has

His method for getting the message to destitute spirits. Gospel broadcasting has gotten behind the bamboo window, the extraordinary mass of China to the general population in China. It has gotten behind the standing framework and achieved hearts in India. By methods for radio communicate, progressively missionary work is being done among these peoples than has been conceivable previously. There is additionally the web, radio, Television, and so forth which make it conceivable to go past the hindrances.

There are individuals somewhere down in transgression (sin), some of them lawbreakers escaping from justice, who have been found by God by methods for gospel radio, web, TV, and so forth. They have been indicted for their wrongdoings (sins) and conveyed to Christ. On the other hand there are religions whose adherents are cautioned by their leaders not to tune in to the gospel, but rather the general population yearn for the things of God, and God is answering them through this open door of radio communicates, transmissions, the web, television broadcasts and so forth.

Dr. John Thomas Wylie

The People Of Little Strength

The Lord in addressing the church in Philadelphia said, "For thou hast a little strength, and hast kept my word, and hast not denied my name."

The world as a rule estimates strength by numbers, however not so with God. He said of the church in Philadelphia that they had a little strength, but they were not really a substantial gathering. The Lord is really speaking to those inside the obvious church who make up the genuine Body of Jesus Christ. He is tending to the individuals who are genuinely conceived of God. In spite of the fact that their number isn't great, He, by the by, accomplishes something for them that is extremely unusual.

We find in reading the first chapter of I Corinthians that there are very few among God's people who are shrewd as men figure wisdom. There are relatively few persuasive, very few who are high conceived. God picked what the world tallies silly to put the wise men to disgrace. God picks what the world include frail or foolish to put strong things to disgrace, shame.

God chooses what the world considers to be poor, weak and immaterial so as to convey its substances to nothing. What's more, the reason in this is no individual will have any reason to brag or boast in God's presence.

Without this assurance I would long ago have ventured out of God's service. In any case, in Him lies all our sufficiency. In Him is all that we need. Without Him we can do nothing (John 15:5 KJV).

There are some who by sheer strength of man power and will power have cut for themselves spots of power and set up incredible governments. In any case, it is to the individuals who have little strength that God says He has opened the door of opportunity and service.

This small and weak group in Philadelphia isn't right just in light of the fact that it is a minority group. There are numerous minority bunches in various exercises and in various lands who aren't right in their points and purposes and direct. The size of the group, regardless of whether incredible or small does not make the group right.

The standard for rightness depends on capabilities other than numbers. Two capabilities are given in this letter which have to do with God's Word and the Person of Jesus Christ. The words are: "Thou hast kept my word, and hast not denied my name." These believers were loyal to the message and loyal to the Person of Jesus Christ.

We have learned from different places in the Word who Jesus truly is. Also, the individuals who don't confess that Jesus Christ is come in the flesh are not of God, but rather are of the spirit of Antichrist. Today there are incredible numbers who have not agreed Christ His legitimate place in their midst. They revere Him as an teacher and praise Him as a man, however, in doing they corrupt, or degrade Him, since He is in all actuality the eternal Son of God who came in human substance to die for men and to rise again from the dead. Jesus Christ is the God-man.

The door has been opened by Christ, not for those to enter who don't confess His proper work and place, but to the individuals who are true with His message and true with His Person.

We should recognize that Christ is everything (our all in all) so far as our life is concerned. In him alone is life, and He is our life as we perused in I John 5 beginning with verse 10: "He that believeth on the Son of God hath the witness in himself: he that believeth not God hath made him a liar; since he believeth not the record that God gave His Son.

What's more, this is the record, that God hath given to us everlasting life, and this life is in His Son. He that hath the Son hath life; and he that hath not the Son of God hath not life."

The assurance to every child of God is this: "I can do all things through Christ which strengtheneth me" (Phil. 4:13 KJV). Victory in the Christian life is in Jesus Christ alone. Is it accurate to say that he is speaking to us? Do we qualify? Have we entered the door that He has opened and no man can shut it?

A Call To Action

What does an open door mean? An open door means an opportunity. It is a call to action. It implies that we will demonstrate our faithfulness to Him through our obedience. Relatively few of God's servants are of the powerful or the mighty of this world however some of them are, as was Paul, for instance. Moses was exceptionally prepared, a man of extraordinary scholarly power and physical power; but there were others again who were obscure and whom the world looked down upon.

In any case, an open door calls for activity (action). God wants us to experience it. Today God has opened up before us the door for world evangelism through radio, TV, web and we must not disappoint Him.

Many a pastor nowadays gets discouraged in light of the fact that it is difficult to inspire, or encourage the unbelievers to come to Christ, not to mention church. Also, regularly revival crusades don't come to the unsaved in the manner in which we might want them to. Believers often disregard chances to come to those unbelievers outwardly, but God still has this open door of broadcasting through which He is reaching the masses.

This is an effectual door which God in His grace has entrusted to us. However I tremble at the responsibility. God will close this door when the assignment is finished or when Christians neglect to go into the open doors displayed.

There was a day in Israel's history when the people who had left Egypt remained on the edge of the promised land at Kadesh-barnea. In any case, they refused to go into Canaan, and God shut that door until thirty-eight years when another generation trusted Him and entered.

The greatest foe of Communism today is the Word of God and the Christ of God. Before the Communist can rule this world, he needs to dispose of Christ and the Bible. It will be vital for Communism to demolish the consciences of men, in light of the fact that through the conscience (inner voice), God goes into men's hearts.

This is the explanation behind Communism's mentally conditioning strategies. They are trying to substitute a mass conscience designed by their fiendish, diabolical leadeers for the individual conscience.

Radio, TV, and the web are the absolute best means now of reaching the masses in their homes, in their shops, in their autos, or wherever they are; for these communicates enter behind each boundary that men may raise.

It can achieve the hungry soul in the formal and dead church, the individual giving up on life, the disappointed and urgent boozer (drunkard), the wayward child, the unchurched, the unreached lands - whatever the circumstance, God can use these communicates of radio, television, and web to reach the hearts of men.

Dr. John Thomas Wylie

We require a spiritual revival in the event that we are to be saved from the surges, the onslaughts and advances of Communism and different tenets that represent a danger to Christianity. We cherish our opportunities, and our freedoms, but they will be saved to us only as we as a nation live in righteousness.

So much that has been said about radio, television, web evangelism can likewise be connected to other open doors. Literature is in like manner one of God's successful techniques. At that point add to that the many time tested strategies for the past ages. God is never without a witness or an open door. A few doors once open are shut today, but new ones have been opened-considerably more effective ways and means than the past ones.

Organized Religious Deception

As opposed to the individuals who have been faithful to Christ we have the individuals who are portrayed as "of the synagogue of Satan." The record is, "Behold, I will make them of the synagogue of Satan, which say they are Jews, and are not, but do lie; behold, I will make them to come and worship before thy feet, and to know that I have loved thee" (Rev. 3:9 KJV).

"Synagogue" implies a gathering or a uniting of individuals, a bringing together of people. The reference was to some organization which professed to be something it was most certainly not.

Information regarding this matter isn't bound to this one verse. In II Corinthians 11:13:15 RSV, an exceptionally solid proclamation is made with references to the individuals who pursue Satan and are double crossers, deceivers proclaiming to be a certain something while they really are something else.

Paul expressed: "For such are false apostles, deceitful workers, transforming themselves into the apostles of Christ. And no marvel; for Satan himself is transformed into an angel of light. Therefore it is no great thing if his ministers also be transformed as the ministers of righteousness; whose end shall be according to their works." These are impostors, disguising their true intent and teaching, behind a false front.

The Apostle Paul dealt with this same organized trickery, deception when he wrote to the Galatians. His words are, "I marvel that you are soon removed from him that called you into the grace of Christ unto another gospel: which is not another; but there be some that trouble you, and would pervert the gospel of Christ" (Gal. 1:6,7 KJV).

The focal point of attack for this situation is simply the gospel, so Paul proceeds: "But though we, or an angel from heaven, preach any gospel unto you than that which we have preached unto you, let him be accursed. As we said previously, so say I now again, If any man preach any other gospel unto you than ye have received, let him be accursed" (vv. 8,9).

The Strategy of Satan does not differ much from age to age. He assaults, attacks if conceivable, the Person of Christ and the good news of Christ. Right now we have religious organizations loaded with religious intensity whose educators and evangelists asserts that everybody is an offspring of God.

They don't qualify the statement as does the Word of God which says, "We are all children of God by faith in Christ Jesus." This demonstrates the children of God are limited to the individuals who are trusting in Christ.

The individuals who preach that all men are children of God are false preachers of the gospel.

"Church" signifies "called out ones" and speaks of people called out from the mass of humanity. God's church does not include everybody on the earth though His gospel made arrangement or provision for all.

Only the people who receive the gospel become part of His true Church. The people who pretend to be Christians have a place with "the synagogue of Satan." Some day such pretending people will recognize and acknowledge that the true followers of Jesus Christ are loved by God.

Jesus Christ Is The Way

When Jesus Christ came to this world He didn't come to demonstrate to us the best way to God. He, Himself, is that way. He expressed in John 14:6, "I am the way, the truth, and the life: no man cometh unto the Father, but by me." He is the Way, not simply the way shower.

In keeping in touch with the Corinthians Paul characterized the gospel in these few words: "Besides, brethren, I declare unto you the gospel which I preached unto you, which also you have received, and wherein ye stand; By which also ye are saved, if ye keep in memory what I have preached unto you, unless ye have believed in vain. For I delivered unto you first of all that which I also received, how that Christ died for our sins according to the scriptures; And that he was buried, and that he rose again the third day according to the scriptures" (I Cor. 15:1-4 ASV).

Various components are outstanding in this passage. Most importantly, this was a message to be received by men. Certain people at Corinth received it and were saved. The First fact they rested on was that Christ died for the sins of men according to the Scriptures.

This speaks about His substitutionary death, the purpose of which was to reconcile us to God. The fact that He was buried demonstrates the removing of our sin; and the fact that He rose again from the dead and is now alive shows that His sacrifice was acceptable before God.

Through His death we are reconciled to God, and we are saved by His resurrection life. This, to sum things up, is the gospel.

A Special Promise

A special promise is made to the church in Philadelphia: "Since thou hast kept the word of my patience, I likewise will keep thee from the hour of temptation, which shall come upon all the world, to try them that dwell upon the earth" (v. 10). Two actualities are imperative here.

One is that an hour of trial is coming upon the earth. The second is that God has promised to keep the believers of the Philadelphia church with the goal that they won't go through that trial. Another interpretation of the condition, "I also will keep thee from the hour of temptation," is, "I also will keep thee out of the hour of temptation."

The believer isn't to be preserved through water as was Noah but is to be removed from the world as was Enoch. Enoch was translated so that he should not see death.

The specific trial that is referenced here is, point of fact, the Tribulation spoken of in numerous parts of the Bible. In Jeremiah 30:7 we have the promise concerning Israel: "Oh! for that day is great, so that none is like it: it is even the time of Jacob's trouble, but he shall be saved out of it."

A part of Israel that will be saved from the scorn, hatred of Satan and the hatred of the Antichrist will be expelled into a desert put for safe-keeping (Rev. 12:14). This, be that as it may, is not the same promise made to the Philadelphia church.

Dr. John Thomas Wylie

Another Scripture dealing the time of Tribulation is Daniel 12:1 KJV. There we read: "And at that time shall Michael stand up, the great prince which standeth for the children of thy people: and there shall be a time of trouble, such as never was since there was a nation even to that same time: and at that time thy people will be delivered, every one that shall be found written in the book."

Israel will be kept through this time of Tribulation just as Noah was kept through the time of the flood. But, the church will be kept out of the Tribulation similarly as Enoch was translated from the earth.

Another word to describe this getaway of the church from what is coming on the earth is given in I Thessalonians 4:13-18. It is verse 17 which gives us the data: "Then we which are alive and remain will be caught up (snatched away) together with them in the clouds, to meet the Lord in the air; and so shall we ever be with the Lord. KJV"

Those believers who have died in Christ will come back with Christ and receive their resurrection bodies; and those of us who are alive on the earth when the Lord comes will be translated or snatched away into His presence having been transformed.

So at that point, Israel, or possibly a specific portion of Israel will be preserved in the midst of the Tribulation and its extremely severe judgments and persecutions. The Church, then again, is removed from (taken out of) this world and consequently kept from that hour of world-wide testing.

The eighteenth verse in this section in I Thessalonians admonishes us to "comfort one another with these words." There would be no comfort if there was a thought of going through the Tribulation and no promise of preservation in it. That preservation is promised for Israel but no such promise is given us.

Be that as it may, none is required, for we are to be kept out of it and won't see it. A considerable lot of us would be slanted to pray if we believe that we were to go through the Tribulation: "Gracious, Lord Jesus kindly don't come until after I have passed on for then I won't have to go into the tribulation and die a shocking death because of those individuals who will be working destruction among thy people at that time."

The coming of the Lord Jesus would be no comfort to the believers of this age if they were faced with a tribulation as opposed to His coming. Why ask, "Master Jesus come rapidly," if going before that coming must be this time of Jacob's trouble? We realize God dependably gives His people grace for any trial they should confront, however that isn't the issue before us in this inquiry. We are advised to look not for a period of tribulation but rather for the coming of the Lord Jesus and to be comforted in the promise of His return.

The Lord promises, "Behold, I come quickly: hold that fast which thou hast, that no man take thy crown."

Chapter Eight

Jesus Christ Speaks To Laodicea

"AND UNTO THE ANGEL of the church of the Laodiceans write; These things saith the Amen, the faithful and true witness, the beginning of the creation of God; I know thy works, that thou art neither cold nor hot: I would thou wert cold or hot. So then because thou art lukewarm, and neither cold nor hot, I will spue thee out of my mouth.

Because thou sayest, I am rich, and increased with goods, and have need of nothing; and knowest not tht thou art wretched, and miserable, and poor, and blind, and naked; I counsel thee to buy of me gold tried in the fire, that thou mayest be rich; and white raiment, that thou mayest be clothed, and that the shame of thy nakedness do not appear; and anoint thine eyes with eyesalve, that thou mayest see. As many as I love, I rebuke and chasten: Be zealous therefore, and repent."

"Behold, I stand at the door, and knock: if any man hear my voice, and open the door, I will come in to him, and will sup with him, and he with me. To him that overcometh will I grant to sit with me in my throne, even as I also overcame, and am set down with my Father in his throne. He that hath an ear, let him hear what the Spirit saith unto the churches" (Rev. 3:14-22 RSV).

The letter to this church should make us look through our hearts. When we see history rehashing itself in the church today with its torpidity and lack of concern, we may well inquire as to whether we are hot, chilly, or lukewarm.

Jesus Christ The Amen

The Lord Jesus describes Himself to this church as the "Amen." This is anything but another title. Paul alluded to it when he kept in touch with the Corinthians: "For all the promises of God in him are yea, and in him Amen, unto the glory of God by us" (1:20 RSV). "Amen" is an untranslated Hebrew word meaning something that is established, something beyond any doubt, and positive. We are to use it at the finish of our petitions where it conveys the importance of "so be it."

In this passage in Revelation, in any case, it is a title given to the Lord Jesus Christ and implies that He is the Final Word and the Truth. It doesn't mean merely that He teaches the word or that He explains the truth, but that He is the Word and the Truth. In Him the promises of God are fulfilled and through Him the judgments of God are to be exercised.

He is the Truth from whom there can be no intrigue. There will be no higher court than the one over which He presides. His word is final, and nothing can be added to it or subtracted from it when He speaks. The finality of authority is His.

It is simply because of God's longsuffering that He doesn't strike men down now when they negate the Lord who has spoken from paradise. God isn't willing that any ought to die, along these lines, for that lost soul that might be reached with the gospel here in this land or in some heathen land, God withholds judgment.

Be that as it may, if we read the iconic issues aright, the season of God's longsuffering may before long be finished and judgment will come. Men can take a look at the sun and the sky and advise whether the day to come will be reasonable or stormy, but they don't peruse the iconic issues accurately except if they read them in the light of Bible prophecy.

The every day news forces upon us the way that the time is gravitating toward when Christ will come. We are starting to see the diminish blueprints of the occasions. We have seen the developments of the northern powers in Russia and her satellite countries. In Europe the development of the old Roman Empire is propelling relentlessly; and there are developments in the east that recommend the joining of the kings of the east may not be far away (If not already joined together).

These are cautioning signs, similar to the shriek of a train out yonder, but they should alarm and warn us concerning what is coming.

Jesus Christ The Faithful And True Witness

Jesus Christ isn't only described as the "Amen" but also as the Faithful and True Witness. In Hebrews God reveals to us that He spoke at various occasions and in many different ways in days gone by unto the fathers by the prophets.

In these last days He has spoken unto us by His Son whom He "hath appointed heir of all things, and by whom also he made the worlds:

Who being the brightness of his glory, the express image of his person, and upholding all things by the word of his power, when he had by himself purged our sins, sat down on the right hand of the Majesty on high" (Heb 1:1-3 KJV).

It is this exalt up One who speaks and withholds no truth essential to our knowledge and direction in this world. He speaks absolute truth which can't be effectively nor successfully contradicted.

He strips the Laodicean church of all its false appearances and cases. They had a form of Christianity which evidently established a profound connection on the shallow scholars of that age. Be that as it may, Christ saw through their whole deceptive front and described them for what they were. In describing this church Christ neither limited nor misrepresented their wrongdoing (sin).

Sardis couldn't conceal itself from this One who knows all things; neither could Ephesus. He knew every one of their works just as He knows all our actions, exercises, plans, activities and intentions.

Christ The Creator

He is also called the beginning of the creation of God. God began everything through Him.

This does not mean He was the first to be created but that He was the member from the Godhead through whom creation appeared. He is the image of the invisible God, the firstborn of every creature. All things were made by Him and for Him. He is before all things and by Him all things hold together.

He speaks with power above that of a prophet, priest, or king. He speaks as the direct representative of the Triune God. His power, His authority is above all that the eye can see or the mind can envision. He is the Creator of the landscape, of the bloom that develops on the slope, of the anxious sea, of the melody of the songbird, of the sun which to us rises and sets in the heavens, of the Spring that overrides the Winter, and the Autumn that pursues the Summer. They are for the most part subject to Him. He it is Who has unparalleled glory, majesty and dignity, and Who speaks in solemn measured tones concerning the church of Laodicea.

A Self-Deceived People

This letter was written to people who were living in profound numbness, spiritual ignornace of their own actual condition. Their outward appearance looked great to them as it did to the world. Be that as it may, a family picture postured for an exceptional event does not inform all concerning the family. The heart condition isn't caught by camera.

The image this church had of itself is disclosed in the words, "because thou sayest." But their true condition is revealed in our Savior's words, "I know thy works." Their genuine condition was in startling differentiation to what they viewed themselves as. They were not cold or hot, but rather lukewarm.

The progress of decline in the diverse churches is exceptionally revealing. To the church at Ephesus the Lord stated, ":Thou hast left thy first love." This demonstrates their motive in service was wrong. The church at Pergamos had in it those who held to the doctrine of Balaam, but church discipline with regard to the false teachers was not excercised. Thyatira demonstrates to us a church ailing, lacking in conviction and that allowed a prophetess to bring idolatry into their midst.

Pergamos had a name that it lived, however it was dead. Be that as it may, Laodica was basically inaccessible. They were not cold, which would mean articulate apathy to the things of Christ on their part; but nor was there the hot, enthusiastic enthusiasm for the things of Christ. They were lukewarm.

Cold

This condition of coldness, to which the Lord alludes, is a negative condition inferring the nonappearance of warmth, proposing something untouchable by the power of God's grace. It could mean the individuals who, in the event that they had heard the gospel, had made no profession of faith with regard to it.

There are many such today who make no affectation of favoring the good news of Christ or of even to such an extent as focusing on it. Such people stand standoffish from the church and every single Christian affiliation. The cases of God are neglected and no endeavor is made to conform to the offer of the gospel.

God and His work are disregarded, and the people associated with this condition are dead in trespasses and sins with the anger (wrath) of God abiding on them.

Hot

Interestingly is the condition of being "hot." Just what is meant here can be clarified by delineations. For instance, Zacchaeus at first was cold to profound things. He carried on with a wicked life and was loathed by his kindred Jews in light of his lead and position as an tax gatherer. Be that as it may, when the love for Jesus Christ went into his heart, separating his resistance and conveying him to salvation, Zacchaeus turned into another man. The enthusiasm of his newly discovered faith is found in his creation compensation to those he had victimized.

Another extraordinary precedent, conceivably the most remarkable in all Scripture, is Saul of Tarsus. He was angry in his animosity toward Christians, and cold toward the things of Christ.

In any case, abandoned his contempt of Christians to love for them and to a commitment to Christ unparalleled in history of the Christian church. He served Christ with an authentic energy and a genuineness that no arrangement of conditions could cause to end up cold.

We see a similar warmth of commitment in Moses who chose rather to endure the sufferings of the general population of God than to utilize the delight of wrongdoing (sin) for a season. At that point there are the prophets, and the witnesses, the saints, yes to be sure, thousands in each age who have neglected insidiousness for righteousness nature in Christ, and have consumed in their own deepest creatures with the longing to live to the glory and honor of the Savior.

Lukewarmness

Between these two conditions, one which plainly portrays spiritual death and the other which obviously shows spiritual life, there is a moderate state depicted here as "lukewarm." This portrays the individuals who had given an incomplete acceptance to the claims of the gospel.

The graces of God had evidently established some impression on them. They may have taken on the the name Christian, and unquestionably they moved toward becoming members of a church, for they were members of the Laodicean church. They may have finished all the outward forms of church congruity; yet there is something lacking, something that shows they don't belong to the Body of Jesus Christ.

It might be that they lack a comprehension and faith in a portion of the imperative teachings identifying with Christianity. Maybe they were happy with the possibility that if individuals were great, and temperate, and kind, as indicated by all accounts on these things, that such was adequate. They were conceivably apathetic or indifferent regarding vital doctrines, for example, the atonement of Jesus Christ, His virgin birth, His deity, and others.

Or then again it may even have been that they had a decent handle of doctrine and were sticklers for orthodoxy; however their kind of living was, for example, to indicate that they have no real life within them. It could represent some who have been persuaded of the truthfulness of the claims of Christianity however have never made a full surrender to Jesus Christ.

It might incorporate some who are divided between their living for God and living for self. They attempt to serve God and mammon at the same time. Their warmth of devotion is killed by the coldness of worldliness to where they are "lukewarm."

Some will even disclose to us that they are zealous, evangelical, however, not evangelistic.

That is certifiably not a legitimate refinement. An outreaching individual is one who trusts that man in his unique state is demolished and that only through redemption in Christ can man be brought back to God.

As a result, the person who is evangelical trusts he has a responsibility to lost people. To be otherwise is to be a double crosser, a traitor to Jesus Christ, and will result in "lukewarmness" as it is exhibited here in Revelation chapter 3.

An unbelieving instructor once stated, "If I accepted what you Christians trust, I could never rest day or night until the point when I had educated all men concerning Christ."

In the lukewarm state, one doesn't have feelings that influence their conscience, the heart, or the will. The principle of the cross isn't really denied, but it isn't viewed as vital. A cross may even be worn as a decoration, however it makes no difference to the wearer so far as its scriptural significance is concerned. Such a one has never been crucified with Christ.

This person may effectively concede that he is a sinner, but there is no hatred for sin. The gross sinner might be felt sorry for by this person, but he makes no effort to reach the deep-dyed sinner for Christ. Certain parts of wrongdoing (sin) might be viewed as frightful, or fearful by the persons who are lukewarm, but sin isn't found in its true character as it is before God. Also, no consideration is paid to the way that judgment will fall upon the unrepentant sinner.

Lukewarmness is the worst noticeably bad express a person could be in. Something should be possible for a "cool" individual, however the lack of concern of the lukewarm is difficult to shake and makes him difficult to reach.

Saul of Tarsus was an incredible sinner, but legitimate in his wrong dispositions and activities, and something should be possible for him once he was demonstrated what the fact of the matter was. Be that as it may, when a man feels himself to be high minded and right, the cases of God don't stir him and convert him. He hates any proposal that he needs repentance or regeneration. He may even be a leader in a church organization but "unsaved."

For a man to be lukewarm is a solid sign that he isn't saved, but in addition that he is vain and will be difficult to move from his spiritual lack of interest. There is more to seek after the salvation of an absolute nonbeliever than for a vain and self-deluded religionist. The publican and the prostitute can be more promptly brought into the kingdom than the hypocritical and glad Pharisee.

There is perhaps nothing so sickening as that which is not one or the other "cool" nor "hot," regardless of whether it is nourishment or drink, or a man's spiritual state. A smug individual, sufficiently warm to be agreeable in his aloofness to the things of God, and who considers daintily the admonitions of the Lord, is lukewarm.

In the light of what we are thinking about concerning this church, only the Lord Jesus Christ could be humane under such conditions. Yet, He cherishes the Laodiceans similarly as He has loved all men. His words, however serious, originate from a heart that was broken for them.

Laodiceans Of Yesterday And Today

This church was smug on the grounds that its people were rich and expanded with products and felt they had need of nothing. It was a church that felt secure in its plenitude of belonging, a kind of security in its wealth of belonging, a sort of security which frequently makes individuals overlook God.

I heard a preacher say at one time, "God, give us a greater amount of the individuals who are poor in the merchandise of this world, rich in Thee, but not really the people who are only wealthy in the matter of material things."

At times we are slanted to wish that there were many who might back Christian work with their millions, but by one way or another God has managed the individuals who have nearly nothing or sufficiently only of this present world's products to deal with their very own and their families' needs and to keep the work of Lord going.

The church of Laodicea thought it had need of nothing. It was free of Divine help. It took pride in its belonging, its property, its association, its people, and envisioned that all was well with it.

What a difference to this is the church at Smyrna concerning which the Lord stated: "I know thy works, and tribulation, and poverty, (but thou art rich)."

What more prominent commendation and honor might one be able to ask than this? The Laodicean frame of mind is normal today. There are individuals who enlighten us not to speak regarding the necessities of the world-that such needs will deal with themselves. When we present an intrigue for missions, such people wind up aggravated, not valuing the extraordinary need on the planet, since they don't know about their very own spiritual need.

Of such Jesus says, as He did to the congregation at Laodicea, thou "knowest not that thou art wretched and miserable, and poor, and blind, and naked." When the Lord said they were wretched He implied that they were not fulfilled. Their wealth couldn't give fulfillment but turned into an abusive weight to them.

Rather than their riches helping them, it ruined their spiritual life and degraded them. We regularly talk about a man being troubled by obligations, but these were loaded by their wealth.

They were miserable, which implies that they were in an abandoned state. Their condition was, for example, to move the heart of our Savior with compassion for them. The individuals who are so insensible of their own spiritual condition that they see no need of life in Christ ought to be objects of our profound concern.

"Poor" as utilized here by the Lord implies that the Laodiceans were homeless people who begged. They didn't generally have what they needed, and they would need to go out somewhere to request it. They felt that material wealth were certifiable riches, however they found from what the Savior said that these wealth just made them beggars. What they had in material riches was not worth having in contrast with what they were dismissing in spiritual things.

The Lord described them at long last as being "visually impaired, blind" They saw nothing obviously. They were partially blind and couldn't get a reasonable picture of what they saw. There are the individuals who reveal to us today that we should be progressive, trusting that they themselves are tolerant, while really they are restricted to exceptionally limit restrains in their point of view.

Their idea of life isn't sufficiently broad enough to see that God has something good for them. Lacking discernment, lacking wisdom, lacking light and clear vision, they come up short on the very essence of life.

Our Savior likewise described them as being naked, implying that they were nude or deprived of apparel. Obviously, from the material viewpoint they, most likely, were dressed richly and perfectly, however profoundly they were down and out. They came up short of the glory of the Lord Jesus Christ.

It was after Adam and Eve had sinned that they saw they were stripped. Preceding this they were evidently dressed in the Shekinah glory of God which secured them similarly as with a piece of clothing of light. However, the minute they trespassed (sinned), that glory withdrew, for they had missed the mark concerning the glory of God.

Our Lord's Appeal

The Savior's attitude toward the Laodiceans was one of love for needy souls. It is the same today as we live in this Laodicean age. As our Lord directed with that church somewhere in the range of 2,000 years ago, He currently counsels with those of our own day who are lukewarm, smug, mollified with their very own things, trusting they are rich when really they are destitute of works that please God, despising the new birth, and disdaining to come to Jesus Christ to receive life from His hands.

"Come and buy" is His counsel to the Laodiceans of any day and age. In any case, if any such would get what He offers, they should come having no cash, and get what is without cost. They should come as homeless people and get from His hand what can't be bought with the gold of this earth.

The Laodicean church was situated in a rich community. That territory was potentially the best business community for black wool in the world. The vendors additionally managed in garments and salves and fragrances, with the goal that huge numbers of the general population were well off, and being affluent anticipated that would pay huge totals for the extravagances of life.

Be that as it may, Jesus came to them and stated, "I have business to do with you, a bigger business than you are doing now. Check out yourselves, and perceive how you remain with reference to heavenly treasure. All you have so far is for this world, and you have been happy with that, demonstrating no worry for your future."

There is no expectation for one outside the church who is cold toward the things of God than for those within who need spiritual life but don't know about it and happy with their condition.

By the by, their case isn't sad in the event that they will listen in to what God needs to say.

God says to purchase of Him, but that is an invitation to come and get a gift from Him. The salvation He gives is based on an unconditional present which no man can legitimacy or buy.

However there is a cost to be paid for one who wishes to get such a salvation. There will be simply the renouncing of self-righteousness and self-sufficiency, and the humbling of the heart to get God's free gift. Such is a huge cost to some who are wealthy in this present world's products, wealthy in grandiosity and in vanity.

This isn't just a message for the individuals who might be satisfied with common things, but for the individuals who might attempt gain common things despite the fact that they have next to none of them. The poor in heart can come effortlessly before God since he realizes he has nothing in the first place. Be that as it may, the independent or self-sufficient must pay the cost of dropping all pride.

At that point they are advised to come to God and get gold-paradise's gold, gold that has been tried in the fire, talking about relationship and fellowship with God. This gold has to do with that which is certifiable and which will stand the test of eternity.

Dr. John Thomas Wylie

White clothing additionally is to be had for coming. This is something to cover the disgrace and exposure of an evil, vain life. Men who may seem sharp looking before the world are stripped naked spiritually before God, with nothing to cover the wrongdoing (sin) or the disgrace, shame. Be that as it may, If they will turn to Jesus Christ they will receive His garment of righteousness to cover them completely.

At that point the appeal is made to purchase eyesalve. This is somewhat balm which will open visually impaired eyes (blind eyes) with the goal that they will perceive what true riches are and what God considers essential. Such a balm will clear up a sinner's spiritual vision to where he sees himself to be as he is and will see unmistakably the offer of redemption in Jesus Christ.

So here we have the picture of Jesus Christ's last appeal to the churches, and we find Him on the inside, but rather outside knocking and asking admission.

Jesus Christ's Last Plea To The Church

This is one of the saddest pictures in all the Bible. Jesus Christ is outside of the professing church pleading for entrance. The strict interpretation of this passage is, "Behold, I have taken my stand at the door, and am knocking." This is an activity going on today. He continues knocking, for sorted out Christendom is in numerous quarters energized with a same soul that characterized the husbandmen in the story of Luke 20:9-18 KJV. By and by we see where men have assumed control or taken over what rightly belongs to God.

A equally heart-searching message is here also for the individual Christian. This tender but delicate request isn't expressed in the voice of the Judge of Revelation 20, yet originates from our High Priest's heart of love for His blood-bought people. Jesus needs to impart the best of paradise's endowments to His own. The steadiness of this love is confirmed or evidenced by the fact, as we have noted previously, that He continues knocking.

Is it accurate to say that we are among the individuals who have received salvation from Him but then have defied and rebelled surrendering our everything to Him? Instead of His finding an open heart, would he say he is stood up to with a closed door? Having readily acknowledged discharge (release) from wrongdoing's (sin's) guilt and embraced the assurance of paradise, would we say we are yet rejecting or refusing Him access to various areas of our regular day to day lives?

He wants to share with us glories far above anything we could ask or think; but the latch is on our side of the door; He won't force His benefits on any of us.

He promises to come in and sup with us. Of this Ottman has expressed: "A dinner is a night supper, it is the last taken before the morning breaks and the day first lights. It is since a long time ago the apostle stated, "The night is far spent, the day is at hand'; to sup with Christ before morning breaks is a foretaste of the coming glory...of heaven."

The time is growing short, and by keeping Him on the outside we are presently missing the best He has for us. Let us make a full and happy surrender to Him. We will find as John expressed in his first epistle: "Truly our fellowship is with the Father and with His Son Jesus Christ."

Bibliography

Epps, T. H. (1`982) Present Labor And Future Rewards: The Believer, His Sin, Conduct, And Rewards. Lincoln, NE.: Back To The Bible Publishers

LaHaye, T. & Parker, T. (2014) The Book Of Revelation Made Clear (International Edition): A Down-To-Earth Guide To Understanding The Most Mysterious Book Of The Bible. Nashville, TN.: Thomas Nelson Publishers

Larkin, C. (1919, 2006) The Book Of Revelation. Glenside, PA.: New York, NY.: Cosimo, Inc., Old Chelsa Station, Reverend Clarence Larkin Estate

Ramsay, W. M. (2016) The Letters To The Seven Churches: A History Of The Early Church. Grand Rapids, MI.: Baker Book House, Endeavor Compass

Welton, J. (2015) Understanding The Seven Churches of Revelation (1st Ed). Rochester, NY.: Welton Academy Biblica, Inc.

Williams, C. B. (1972) The New Testament: A Translation In The Language Of The People. Chicago, Ill.: Moody Publisher Press

The Combined bible Dictionary And Concordance (1984) Dallas, TX.: American Evangelistic Association

The Holy Bible (1964) Authorized King James Version. Chicago, Ill.: J. G. Ferguson

The Holy Bible (1953) The Revised Standard Version. Nashville, TN.: Thomas Nelson & Sons (Used By Permission)

The Holy Bible (1901) The American Standard Version. Nashville, TN.: Thomas Nelson (Used By Permission)

The Holy Bible (1959) The Berkeley Version. Grand Rapids, MI.: Zondervan (Used By Permission)

About the Author

THE REVEREND DR. JOHN Thomas Wylie is one who has dedicated his life to the work of God's Service, the service of others; and being a powerful witness for the Gospel of Our Lord and Savior Jesus Christ. Dr. Wylie was called into the Gospel Ministry June 1979, whereby in that same year he entered The American Baptist College of the American Baptist Theological Seminary, Nashville, Tennessee.

As a young Seminarian, he read every book available to him that would help him better his understanding of God as well as God's plan of Salvation and the Christian Faith. He made a commitment as a promising student that he would inspire others as God inspires him. He understood early in his ministry that we live in times where people question not only who God is; but whether miracles are real, whether or not man can make a change, and who the enemy is or if the enemy truly exists.

Dr. Wylie carried out his commitment to God, which has been one of excellence which led to his earning his Bachelors of Arts in Bible/Theology/Pastoral Studies. Faithful and obedient to the call of God, he continued to matriculate in his studies earning his Masters of Ministry from Emmanuel Bible College, Nashville, Tennessee & Emmanuel Bible College, Rossville, Georgia. Still, inspired to please the Lord and do that which is well – pleasing in the Lord's sight, Dr. Wylie recently on March 2006, completed his Masters of Education degree with a concentration in Instructional Technology earned at The American Intercontinental University, Holloman Estates, Illinois. Dr. Wylie also previous to this, earned his Education Specialist Degree from Jones International University, Centennial, Colorado and his Doctorate of Theology from The Holy Trinity College and Seminary, St. Petersburg, Florida.

Dr. Wylie has served in the capacity of pastor at two congregations in Middle Tennessee and Southern Tennessee, as well as served as an

Evangelistic Preacher, Teacher, Chaplain, Christian Educator, and finally a published author, writer of many great inspirational Christian Publications such as his first publication: *"Only*

One God: Who Is He?" – published August 2002 via formally 1ˢᵗ books library (which is now AuthorHouse Book Publishers located in Bloomington, Indiana & Milton Keynes, United Kingdom) which caught the attention of The Atlanta Journal Constitution Newspaper.

Dr. Wylie is happily married to Angel G. Wylie, a retired Dekalb Elementary School teacher who loves to work with the very young children and who always encourages her husband to move forward in the Name of Jesus Christ. They have Four children, 11 grand-children and one great-grandson all of whom they are very proud. Both Dr. Wylie and Angela Wylie serve as members of the Salem Baptist Church, located in Lilburn, Georgia, where the Reverend Dr. Richard B. Haynes is Senior pastor.

Dr. Wylie has stated of his wife: "she knows the charm and beauty of sincerity, goodness, and purity through Jesus Christ. Yes, she is a Christian and realizes the true meaning of loveliness as the reflection as her life of holy living gives new meaning, hope, and purpose to that of her husband, her children, others may say of her, "Behold the handmaiden of the Lord." A Servant of Jesus Christ!

Printed in the United States
By Bookmasters